About This Bo

A New Kind of Creative Pr
Artificial Intelli

In late August of 2023, I started playing around with a tool, Code Interpreter, released by OpenAI.

For those who don't know, you talk to Code Interpreter (it has recently been given the more bland name, Data Analysis). And it codes for you in Python. It will merge datasets; do sophisticated calculations; and produce charts and graphs.

To say that I was blown away would be an understatement. Code Interpreter was the most amazing thing that I had ever encountered to that point, topping my previous top 5: the iPhone, Rao's marinara sauce, Bruce Springsteen concerts, Yankees playoff games, and sex.

With Code Interpreter, things that used to take me three months of work now took me three hours – or sometimes less.

Within a couple of months, I had a realization. As a non-fiction book author who analyzes data, Code Interpreter meant nothing less than a complete revolution in my creative process. All of my previous calculations on how long a creative project should take were out the window.

If the average analysis took 1/720 of the time it used to take, then how long should it take me to write a book?

I suspected that I could now write a book in roughly 30 days of intense work. I challenged myself to do so. And I have now done it.

For context, I have previously written two books, *Everybody Lies* and *Don't Trust Your Gut*. Each took me about 3 years of full-time work.

To be fair, and to avoid over-claiming, in writing this book, I relied on some studies that I had previously done on the genetics of basketball talent and the demographics of basketball talent. Also, I spent a couple of months playing around with some AI tools to learn how they worked. I did, during that period, try these tools out on some NBA stats. And I have spent the better part of a lifetime thinking about the topics of this book. Finally, my dad has recently retired from his job as a journalism professor and is obsessed with basketball and was willing to work editing this book. Thanks, dad!

But the bulk of the work for this book – including a lot of new research on basketball – took roughly 30 days. By any calculation, this book was produced in a shockingly short period of time.

Every chart that you see in this book was made by ChatGPT's Data Analysis. Every piece of art was created by AI – either DALL·E or Midjourney. Some of the text was written with assistance from ChatGPT.

In a book that relied so much on AI, I should make one quick note about truth. There have been some much-publicized examples of ChatGPT hallucinating and making up facts. You might wonder about the accuracy of a book that relied so heavily on AI. Indeed, among a few people I sent a draft of this book to, one of the top comments has been "This seems amazing. Are the stats true?"

The answer is a definitive yes. To be clear, I did not let ChatGPT loose to write material and potentially hallucinate. Instead, I used ChatGPT to write code, which I then always went over closely. All remaining errors, which I suspect are few, are due to me, not ChatGPT. I believe that this book contains many new, true, and fundamental insights into the game of basketball.

While reading this book, you may wonder how you can best use AI to speed up your work process, as well. I have an Appendix where I give the best tricks that I have learned during this project. I also will be tweeting more learnings. (@SethS_D). If AI has not already totally transformed your work process, you are doing something wrong.

But back to basketball. Have you ever wondered:

- What percent of 7 footers are in the NBA?
- What determines how many basketball players a country produces?
- Just how genetic is basketball talent?
- What, besides genes, do NBA-playing parents pass on to their kids?
- How does socioeconomic status impact your chances of reaching the top of basketball?
- What determines who is a great clutch shooter?
- Is the NBA draft efficient?
- What do great coaches do?

Wonder no more! You are about to find out the answers to these questions – and many more. Meanwhile, I am on to my next challenge – to, with the help of AI, write 100 more books.

Chapter 1: No Court for Short Men

On a frosty Massachusetts morning in the waning years of the 19th century, James Naismith had a bunch of restless kids to entertain. Naismith, a spry physical educator, looked for tools he might use for a game his students might enjoy.

He rummaged through a closet and found a soccer ball. Could be useful.

He asked a janitor for something to help in his game – perhaps some boxes. The janitor came back with two peach baskets.

"Hmm..." Naismith paced. He looked at the peach baskets. He looked at the ball. He looked at the vicious snow outside.

The most straightforward game – requiring minimal effort on Naismith's part – would have involved placing the baskets on the floor. This would mirror the game Powerball from "American Gladiator", where contestants dodge opponents to drop a ball into a bucket—a game universally loved by participants of every stature.

But, instead, Mr. Naismith made a very different choice, one that would shatter the dreams of countless 5'9" sports enthusiasts, such as me. Naismith nailed the peach baskets to the <u>gym balcony high above the floor.</u>

"Get it in there," Naismith said, pointing way up towards the sky. And this paved the way for seven foot-plus men to become some of the most legendary athletes in history. With one executive decision, Naismith, himself only 5'10 ½", set the demographics of basketball in motion. This would be a tall man's game.

And any study of what it takes to make the NBA has to start with the Big Question: how much does height influence your chances of becoming an NBA player?

Let's dive into the data!

The height of American males is distributed on a bell curve centered around 5'10". Here are the odds of men exceeding various height thresholds:

- 6'0" or above: 25 %
- 6'6" or above: 0.383 % (1 in 261)
- 7'0" or above: 0.00015 % (1 in 653,327)

The average NBA player stands a tad over 6'6". Here are the odds of NBA players exceeding the same height thresholds:

- 6'0" or above: 97 %
- 6'6" or above: 56 %
- 7'0" or above: 5 %

When you put together the full curves of heights of all men and heights of NBA players, you get the chart that follows: the odds of men of every height reaching the NBA.

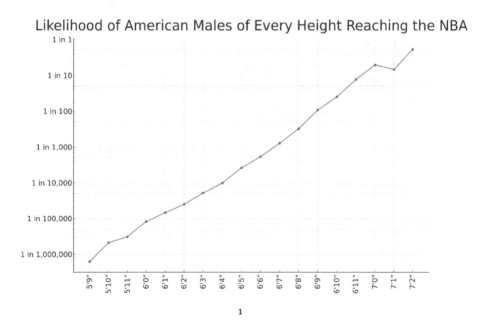

Likelihood of American Males of Every Height Reaching the NBA

Note the strikingly predictable relationship between height and reaching the NBA. Each inch roughly doubles your

---

[1] Notes on the sources of data for all charts are at the end of the book.

chances of making the NBA – throughout the height distribution. A 6'1" man has roughly twice the chance of reaching the NBA as a 6'0" man. A 6'2" man has roughly twice the chance of reaching the NBA as a 6'1" man ... A 7'0" man has roughly twice the chance of reaching the NBA as a 6'11" man. And so on. (The dip at 7'1" is almost certainly due to noise.)

This means that your probability of reaching the NBA differs drastically depending on your height. The probability of a man of below-average height – under 5'10" – reaching the NBA is 1 in 3.8 million. The probability of a man over 7 feet tall reaching the NBA is roughly 1 in 7.[2]

Further, the enormous value of height in reaching the NBA has massive implications for how the athleticism of NBA players varies with height.

Tall NBA Players Aren't Great Athletes

This is the dirty secret of basketball: Extremely tall basketball players aren't necessarily world-class athletes.

Obviously all professional athletes must be in tip-top shape. But, if men over 7 feet have a 1 in 7 chance of reaching the NBA, this suggests, if you are 7 feet tall, you don't have to have off-the-charts athletic potential to reach the NBA; you just have to be in the top 14 %. Indeed, on every athletic skill that we can measure, tall NBA players are, on average, substantially worse than short NBA players.

Tall NBA players, on average, jump much less high off the ground than short NBA players.[3]

---

[2] Many people have done similar simulations and come up with similar results. I believe the first was Pablo S. Torre, in *Sports Illustrated*, who estimated that 17 % of seven footers between the ages of 20 and 40 in the United States were in the NBA.

[3] You might think that there is some physiological reason that taller people would jump less high. However, I – and other people on Twitter, who brought this up – were unable to find any evidence that height is negatively correlated with vertical leap in the entire population. You might think that taller people would jump less high because they have to carry more weight. However, the

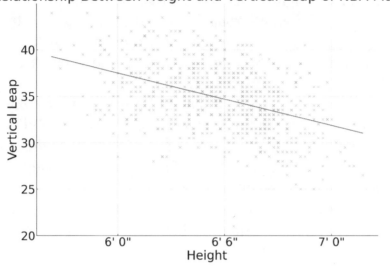

Relationship Between Height and Vertical Leap of NBA Players

Tall NBA players are, on average, far slower than short NBA players.[4]

(negative) impact of height on vertical leap among NBA players remains almost as strong, correcting for a player's weight. I suspect that a lot of the reason many of us think that extremely tall people are inherently worse athletes – less fast, lower vertical jumps, and less coordinated – is because the times we tend to compare really tall people to shorter people are when we watch basketball. And the tallest NBA players are, on average, worse athletes because they don't have to be as good due to their height advantage.

[4] Related to the previous footnote, extreme tallness can be signs of an illness, which can create lots of other problems, which would limit athletic performance. All of the tallest people in history had a condition called giantism, which is caused by an overproduction of growth hormone, usually due to growths in the pituitary gland. Most of these men had major health problems and died young. An example is the tallest man in history, Robert Wadlow, 8'11", who died at the age of 22. The only NBA player I am aware of whose height was brought upon by a disorder was 7'7" Gheorghe Dumitru Mure☐an. Mure☐an's parents were average height, and he grew to his height due to a pituitary gland disorder. Other extremely tall NBA players appear to have reached their height due an extraordinary number of height-enhancing genes. For example, the genome of 7'6" Shawn Bradley was studied and he was found to have 198 genetic variants known to make people taller. Manute Bol, 7'6", came from a family of extremely tall people. (His father was 6'8" and mother was 6'10".) Yao Ming's father was 6'7", and his mother was 6'3".

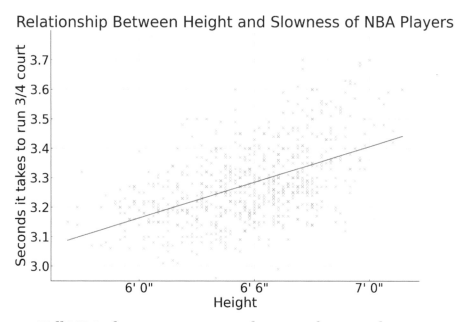

Relationship Between Height and Slowness of NBA Players

Tall NBA players, on average, shoot much worse than short NBA players.

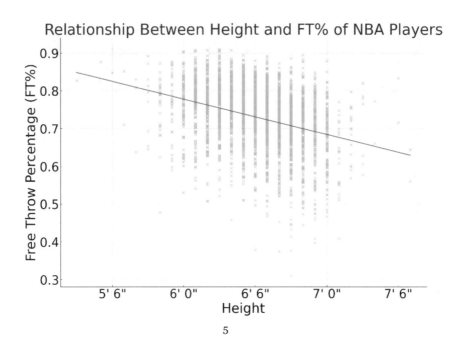

Relationship Between Height and FT% of NBA Players

5

Taller NBA players also have, on average, much worse ability to change direction and a significantly higher percentage of body fat. Further, this shocked me: the average 7 foot-or-above NBA player bench presses less than the average 6 foot-or-below NBA player.[6] Shorter NBA players are frequently stronger than taller NBA players!

Whereas NBA players who are short are all extraordinary, insane athletes, the athletic performance of tall players – apart from those flowing directly from height, such as the ability to dunk a ball – is frequently shockingly pedestrian.

---

[5] In talking to people affiliated with the NBA about this book, some asked whether larger hands, which taller people are likely to have, adversely impact free throw shooting. Notoriously poor free throw shooters Wilt Chamberlain and Shaquille O'Neal are also known for their legendarily big hands, as we will discuss in a later chapter. When you run a regression of free throw percentage on hand size and height, hand size is a statistically significant negative predictor of free throw percentage. But the coefficient on height remains highly significant and of a similar magnitude.

[6] All the physical stats are only among NBA players who were measured at the NBA Draft Combine.

Tall NBA Players Are Way Worse Athletes Than Short NBA Players

	Avg <=6 foot NBA Player	Avg >=7 foot NBA Player
Time to Sprint ¾ Court	3.18 secs	3.54 secs
Vertical Leap	37.5 in.	29.3 in.
Bench Press (185 lbs)	8.6 reps	7.0 reps
Body Fat	6.1 %	8.1 %
Free Throw Shooting	73.9 %	63.1 %
Three-Point Shooting	29.4 %	16.5 %

7

The average 7-foot NBA player has a vertical leap of 29.3 inches. While impressive, this is only a few inches higher than my read of the best estimates of how high an average male with significant training and practice might be able to leap.[8]

The average 7-foot NBA player would run a 100-meter dash in more than 12 seconds. This would be below-average on an average high school track team.

The average 7-foot NBA player shoots free throws at 63 %. This would put them below-average on a random high school basketball team.

Numerous basketball hobbyists can shoot free throws better than 2 of the consensus best NBA players in history: Shaquille O'Neal (7'1") and Wilt Chamberlain (also 7'1").[9]

---

[7] The weighted average for FT% are 79.0 % for those 6 feet or under and 68.8 % for those 7 feet or over, since better free throw shooters tend to attempt more free throws.

[8] Even if 7-foot NBA players only have to have 1 in 7 natural athletic ability to reach the NBA, the fact that they train in basketball all the time makes them far better athletes.

[9] An appropriate self-effacing note while I critique these tall all-time greats. My vertical leap is about 10 inches; I was the slowest person on my freshman baseball team, where my athletic career peaked. And I am a mediocre free

11

For just about any sport, the greats went through a ruthless selection process and have insanely rare talents. Kylian Mbappé Lottin's control of a soccer ball with his feet is a 1 in 1 billion talent. Shohei Ohtani's ability to throw and hit a ball is a 1 in 1 billion talent.

But, for 7-foot-plus NBA players, the normal ruthless selection process for reaching the top of the athletic world doesn't exist.

Who is The Best Height-Adjusted Player of All-Time?

Considering height's supreme importance in basketball, this raises a question that shorter men like me have been asking ourselves for a long time: What if you took height out of the equation? How would basketball players rank?

It turns out – and the math on this is so very neat – you can, rather precisely, answer these questions. You can literally calculate, for any player, how good they are on a height-adjusted basis! And, speaking as a 5'9" (on a good day) basketball enthusiast, I must say, this has been a most enjoyable mathematical adventure.

I will leave the (very cool) math to an Appendix – for those interested. But I was able to create a new stat, which I call MUGGSIES: **M**etric for **U**nderstanding **G**ame, **G**iven **S**porting **I**ndividual's **E**ffectiveness & **S**ize.[10] MUGGSIES measures how many standard deviations above the mean every NBA player is in non-height basketball ability.

Without further ado, here are the Top 10 Height-Adjusted players in NBA history:

---

throw shooter. A self-aggrandizing note: I do have a wicked hook shot, although I found it very hard to get off at 5'9".

[10] I thank ChatGPT for coming up with that backronym … and twitter user Steve Werby for informing me that it was called a backronym.

Top 10 Height-Adjusted Players in NBA History

Rank	Player	Height	MUGGSIES
1	Muggsy Bogues	5'3"	5.77
2	Chris Paul	6'0"	5.70
3	Earl Boykins	5'5"	5.56
4	Spud Webb	5'6"	5.31
5	John Stockton	6'1"	5.25
6	Bill Sharman	6'1"	5.23
7	Calvin Murphy	5'9"	5.20
8	Isaiah Thomas	5'9"	5.19
9	Michael Jordan	6'6"	5.10
10	Jerry West	6'3"	5.06

* MUGGSIES: Can be thought of as Standard Deviations Above the Mean in Non-Height Basketball Ability [11] [12]

Aha! The average height of the top 10 height-adjusted basketball players of all time is 5'10", exactly the same as the average height of the population at large.

And many of the greatest basketball players in history don't look so good when you adjust for height. Let's see the height-adjusted rankings of the top 10 basketball players of all time, according to a recent list by *The Athletic*. The average height of men on this list: 6'11" The average ranking of these top 10 all-time NBA legends when you take out their height: 1,060.

---

[11] Since numerous people have asked, Steph Curry ranks #11. Allen Iverson ranks much lower, in part because, in creating the formula, I am using Win Shares, a statistic which heavily penalizes high-scoring players with low field goal percentages.

[12] The current formula for MUGGSIES does not adjust for the time period in which a player played. In future work, I am considering making such an adjustment, since the average height of an NBA player increased 3 inches between 1947 and 2003. Such an adjustment would hurt Bill Sharman and Jerry West, to the great delight of the numerous Steph Curry fans who have critiqued this chart on Twitter.

Where NBA Legends Rank in Basketball Ability, Taking Out Height

Player	Athletic Ranking of Basketball Ability	Height	POS	Ranking on MUGGSIES (Basketball Ability, Absent Height)
Michael Jordan	1	6'6"	SG	9
LeBron James	2	6'9"	SF	395
Kareem Abdul-Jabbar	3	7'2"	C	2,244
Bill Russell	4	6'10"	C	1,419
Magic Johnson	5	6'9"	PG	269
Wilt Chamberlain	6	7'1"	C	1,778
Larry Bird	7	6'9"	SF	835
Shaquille O'Neal	8	7'1"	C	2,188
Tim Duncan	9	6'11"	C	1,557
Kobe Bryant	10	6'6"	SG	403

And, now, I will use this opportunity, finally writing my treatise on basketball, to (gulp) attack Michael Jordan.

Michael Jordan is considered the consummate basketball player. We are supposed to learn, from him, the lessons of mastering one's craft.

And sure, his basketball skills are ridiculously impressive. Jordan combined his 2.7 standard deviations above-the-mean height with 5.1 standard deviation above the mean basketball skill on his way to 6 championships and 5 MVP Awards.

But is Michael's discipline, work ethic, and overall mastery of his craft more impressive than that of Muggsy?

I – and the numbers – would argue: No! Muggsy is the man who mastered the craft of basketball better than any man who has ever lived. The ceiling for Muggsy's basketball career was always going to be much lower than Michael's. But Muggsy overcame a 2.3 standard deviation below-the-mean height handicap to become a solid NBA player for 14 seasons.

Forget "The Last Dance," the famous documentary about Jordan's attempt to win his 6th championship in the 1997-1998 season? I want "The Last Stand," Muggsy Bogues' 1997-1998 attempt to retain, as a 5'3" man, a starting position for the 10th straight season, despite ferocious competition from Brian Shaw, a man 13 (!) inches taller than him.

Plus, Michael Jordan was kind of an asshole – even to Muggsy. He trash talked Muggsy, calling him "little fella," "little ass," and possibly "midget." These types of stories are part of Michael's legend, supposedly just another part of his competitiveness and drive. But, by the standards of 2023, I think they come across as being a bully and, generally, a dick.

Anyway, I hope these charts can start – and finish – a new debate. I'm tired of debating Michael vs. LeBron vs. Kareem.

When it comes to the best height-adjusted player in NBA history, the debate is Muggsy vs. Chris vs. Earl. And Muggsy wins!

Chapter 2: Missing LeBrons

The best potential basketball player in the world right now is likely working as a rice farmer in India.

I will get to that in a bit. But first, it's time for a very brief history of basketball.

In December 1891, James Naismith, as mentioned in the previous chapter, nailed two peach baskets to gym railings – and had his kids compete to get a ball in the baskets. And basketball was started.

In 1946, businessman Walter Brown, owner of the Boston Garden, looked for a way to fill his arenas on nights in which the hockey team wasn't playing. He partnered with other businessmen to start a league of basketball teams in big cities. And the NBA was started.

In 1948, a 5'11" point guard by the name of Hank Biasatti, hailing from Beano, Italy, with a clever dribble, was invited to an NBA camp; impressed the coaches; and was given a spot on the team. And the internationalization of basketball was started.

Or, sort of. Biasatti played 6 games, quit, and failed to start much of a trend. Through the 1970s, international players were one-off curiosities.

But the increased popularity of the game worldwide – in part due to the clever international marketing of stars like Magic Johnson, Larry Bird, and Michael Jordan – has led to more foreign players each year. The story of basketball in the past 30 years, like the story of the world, is a story of globalization.

Foreign-born men made up 7 percent of NBA players in 1990, including solid players like Dražen Petrović from Croatia, Rik Smits from the Netherlands, and Detlef Schrempf from Germany.

Foreign-born men made up 17 percent of NBA players in 2005, including stars like Dirk Nowitzki from Germany, Tim Duncan from the US Virgin Islands, and Yao Ming from China.

And foreign-born men make up more than 20 percent of NBA players today, including arguably the game's three best:

Nikola Jokić from Serbia, Giannis Antetokounmpo from Greece, and Joel Embiid from Cameroon.

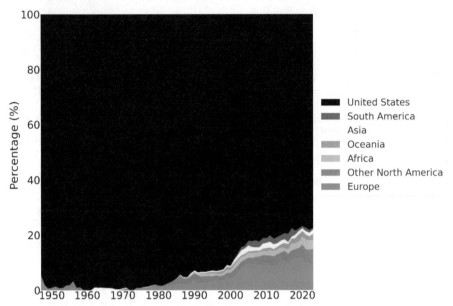

A few countries – Montenegro, the Bahamas, and the US Virgin Islands – now even produce NBA players at a higher per capita rate than the United States does.

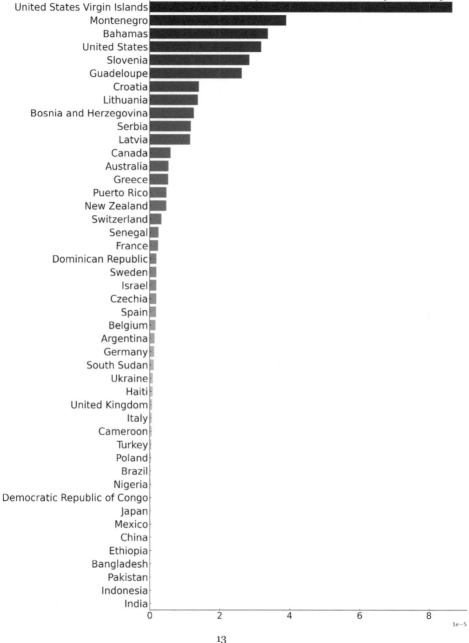

NBA Players per Million Births, by Country

13

19

But, while it is true that players from most countries outside the United States have the best chance they've ever had of reaching the NBA, it is certainly not true that there is anything resembling equality of opportunity for reaching the NBA.

Only three regions of the world produce NBA players at a rate within the same order of magnitude as that of the United States: the Caribbean, the Baltic states, and the former Yugoslavia.

And there are enormous countries in the world that have given us few-or-no NBA players. To see how many "missing" players there are from some parts of the world, consider this thought experiment: What if the demographics of the NBA looked like the demographics of the world? If this were the case, at the start of the 2023-2024 season, there would be:

- 79 players from China
- 78 from India
- 15 from Indonesia
- 14 from Pakistan
- 9 from Bangladesh
- 7 from Mexico
- 6 from the Philippines
- 6 from Egypt
- 6 from Ethiopia
- and 5 from Vietnam.

Instead, these countries will collectively have 0 players on active rosters to start the season.[14]

Why aren't there more NBA players from Mexico and India? Why does Serbia produce so many more players than the Netherlands? Why does Argentina produce players at 3 times

---

[14] While no current NBA players were born in China, China has produced 6 players over the years, most notably the Hall of Famer Yao Ming; this is nowhere near as many as would be expected based on their population size.

the rate that Brazil does? More generally, what determines how many NBA players a country produces?

It turns out that the rate at which countries produce NBA players can be explained almost perfectly by three factors – two obvious and one less so.

1.   Average Height of Males

In the previous chapter, we talked about the enormous advantage that height offers in making the NBA. Which is why it is no surprise that Timor-Leste has never produced an NBA player. This country in southeastern Asia has a mean male height of 5'3" – the shortest in the world.

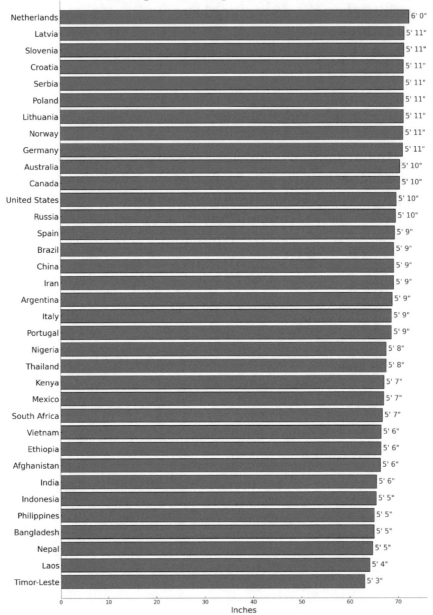

Average Male Height (Selected Countries)

Netherlands	6' 0"
Latvia	5' 11"
Slovenia	5' 11"
Croatia	5' 11"
Serbia	5' 11"
Poland	5' 11"
Lithuania	5' 11"
Norway	5' 11"
Germany	5' 11"
Australia	5' 10"
Canada	5' 10"
United States	5' 10"
Russia	5' 10"
Spain	5' 9"
Brazil	5' 9"
China	5' 9"
Iran	5' 9"
Argentina	5' 9"
Italy	5' 9"
Portugal	5' 9"
Nigeria	5' 8"
Thailand	5' 8"
Kenya	5' 7"
Mexico	5' 7"
South Africa	5' 7"
Vietnam	5' 6"
Ethiopia	5' 6"
Afghanistan	5' 6"
India	5' 6"
Indonesia	5' 5"
Philippines	5' 5"
Bangladesh	5' 5"
Nepal	5' 5"
Laos	5' 4"
Timor-Leste	5' 3"

Inches

Even small differences in mean height translate to large differences in how many people are of extraordinary height. For example, we would expect a country with an average height of

5'11" to have 25 times more 7-footers than a country with an average height of 5'9".

For this reason, the number of NBA players from a country starts exploding when a country's mean male height gets very high – above 5'10".

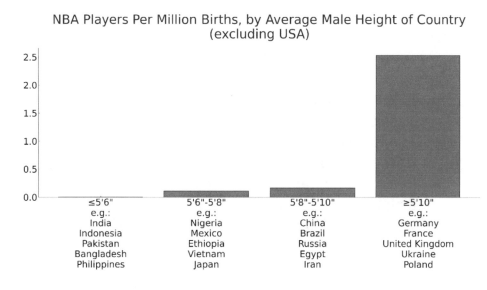

NBA Players Per Million Births, by Average Male Height of Country (excluding USA)

≤5'6"	5'6"-5'8"	5'8"-5'10"	≥5'10"
e.g.:	e.g.:	e.g.:	e.g.:
India	Nigeria	China	Germany
Indonesia	Mexico	Brazil	France
Pakistan	Ethiopia	Russia	United Kingdom
Bangladesh	Vietnam	Egypt	Ukraine
Philippines	Japan	Iran	Poland

Among countries with average male heights at or below 5'6", there has only been one NBA player: Hasheem Thabeet, 7'3", from Tanzania (average male height: 5'5 ½"). And Thabeet was hardly a typical boy from this country. Thabeet was born to an Oxford-educated architect and raised in Dar es Salaam, a city that is much more developed than the rest of the country.[15]

2. Interest in Basketball

If you grow up to be an enormous man – say, 7 foot or above – your potential as a basketball player is not hard to see

---

[15] South Sudan produces more basketball players than most African countries. This is due to the Dinka tribe, who have an average male height over 5'11". Members of the Dinka tribe include Manute Bol (7'6"), Luol Deng (6'9"), and Thon Maker (7'0").

(literally). Perhaps it will be a gym teacher. Or perhaps it's a coach. Or maybe a scout. But, undoubtedly, someone is going to spot you walking down the halls or the street and say "Put a basketball in this man's hand."

In fact, some of history's greatest basketball players didn't even take up the game until they were teenagers – and had a growth spurt.
These include:

- Hakeem Olajuwon, 7'0". Born in Nigeria, he was a soccer goalkeeper before taking up basketball at the age of 15.
- Joel Embiid, 7'0". Born in Cameroon, he played volleyball and soccer before taking up basketball at the age of 15.
- Dikembe Mutombo, 7'2". Born in the Democratic Republic of Congo, he played soccer and practiced martial arts before taking up basketball at the age of 16.

All across the world, 7-foot teenagers are spotted (again, it's easy to do), introduced to, and eventually trained in basketball. Often, these giants make the NBA. With some frequency, they make the NBA Hall of Fame.
If you aren't heads above your fellow countrymen, however, your potential basketball talent may be missed. And it is very likely to be missed if you are born outside the United States. While we are increasingly good at finding very tall basketball talent around the world – and getting them to try the game – we are still terrible at spotting "short" basketball talent outside the United States.

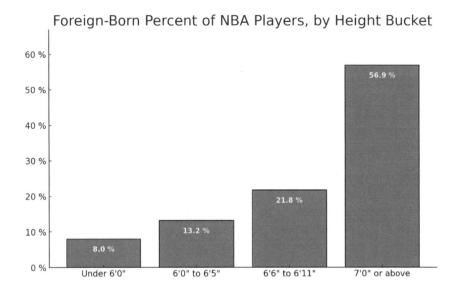

Foreign-Born Percent of NBA Players, by Height Bucket

How many men who had the potential to shoot like Steph Curry instead worked on their family farm in Vietnam? How many men who had the potential to pass like John Stockton instead spent their afternoons playing soccer with their friends? How many men who had the potential to do everything with a basketball, like Calvin Murphy, never even picked one up?

Among shorter potential basketball talent, you need some reason to develop interest in the game – and discover and develop this talent. And just about the only way that shorter people outside the United States play basketball is if they live in one of the small number of regions of the world that love basketball. Indeed, interest in basketball – as measured on Google Trends – is the biggest worldwide predictor of "short" NBA basketball players produced.

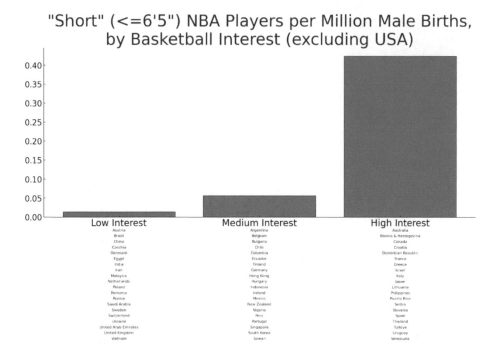

"Short" (<=6'5") NBA Players per Million Male Births, by Basketball Interest (excluding USA)

Low Interest	Medium Interest	High Interest
Austria	Argentina	Australia
Brazil	Belgium	Bosnia & Herzegovina
China	Bulgaria	Canada
Czechia	Chile	Croatia
Denmark	Colombia	Dominican Republic
Egypt	Ecuador	France
India	Finland	Greece
Iran	Germany	Israel
Malaysia	Hong Kong	Italy
Netherlands	Hungary	Japan
Poland	Indonesia	Lithuania
Romania	Ireland	Philippines
Russia	Mexico	Puerto Rico
Saudi Arabia	New Zealand	Serbia
Sweden	Nigeria	Slovenia
Switzerland	Peru	Spain
Ukraine	Portugal	Thailand
United Arab Emirates	Singapore	Türkiye
United Kingdom	South Korea	Uruguay
Vietnam	Taiwan	Venezuela

It is exceedingly rare for a man 6'5" or under born in a country without much interest in basketball to reach the NBA. In fact, the majority of the players who show up in the above chart in the Low Interest category – such as Ben Gordon (born in the United Kingdom) – moved to the United States when they were young. And, among the "short" NBA players who were actually raised in a low-interest basketball country, every single one was raised in an enormous city, where they happened to connect with a basketball organization. Examples include Leandro Barbosa, who competed in the São Paulo State Championship in Brazil's largest city, and Gabriel Lundberg, who competed in 3x3 streetball tournaments in Copenhagen, Denmark.

Why, you might ask, is basketball popular in certain parts of the world and not others? The answer is almost always: seemingly arbitrary decisions from between 80 and 120 years ago.

The three regions in which basketball is most popular are the United States, the Baltic States, and the former Yugoslavia, which is why these regions produce so many NBA players.

Why Basketball is so Popular in the USA

The reason basketball is popular in the United States, as we discussed, is because of James Naismith, who had left his native Canada to attend the YMCA Training School in Springfield, Massachusetts. Naismith's invention on that snowy day gave us Michael Jordan. If Naismith had instead been in England when he had his eureka moment, perhaps some 6'6" man from England would have been history's best (non-height-adjusted) player.

Why Basketball is so Popular in the Baltic States

A reason basketball is popular in the Baltic states is that, shortly before World War II, Lithuania decided that it wanted to build camaraderie among countrymen scattered around the globe. It decided to recruit Lithuanian-born people now living in other countries to compete in sporting events. This included Lithuanian-Americans. Because Americans were the best basketball players in the world, Lithuania won the 1937 EuroBasket title, led by Frank Lubin, the Los Angeles-born son of Lithuanian immigrants. Because it was one of the only times Lithuania had won a major sporting event, Lithuania became obsessed with basketball. Latvia became jealous of Lithuania, and they upped their basketball training. If Lithuania had not invited Americans to compete in the 1937 EuroBasket title, we might not have one of history's greatest big-man passers, Arvydas Sabonis.

Why Basketball is so Popular in the former Yugoslavia

The popularity of basketball in the former Yugoslavia can also be traced back to politics. The communist regime after World War II wanted to use sports to build civic engagement. And they identified basketball as one of the best games to teach the principles of communism: selflessness and teamwork. If the Communists had not succeeded in taking over Yugoslavia after World War II, the NBA likely never would have seen the likes of Dražen Petrović, Peja Stojaković, or Bojan Bogdanović.

3. <u>Interest in Another (Specific) Sport Where Height Matters</u>

On June 22, 2021, in front of scouts from every NBA team, Jericho Sims leaped 44.5 inches. Add this to his measured 106 inches standing reach (Sims is 6'10"). And Jericho Sims got the top of his hands to 150.5 inches – 12 feet, 6 1/2 inches.

Among 1,479 players who have been measured, this was the single highest, topping Tacko Fall, JaVale McGee, and Dwight Howard. Sims has such insane leaping ability, he once bruised his head by hitting the rim on a dunk. Seriously, you can watch a video of this online.[16] Jericho Sims can jump higher than, well, everybody.

Everybody, that is, except for Matey Kaziyski. Kaziyski can leap his hands all the way up to 153.5 inches – – or 12 feet, 9 ½ inches – 3 inches higher than Sims.

But Kaziyski has never tried to block the shots of Fall, McGee, or Howard. He has never seriously tried basketball. Kaziyski, who stands at 6'8", from Bulgaria, is a volleyball player, currently playing for Trentino Volley.

Among countries with similar average heights and similar interest in basketball, interest in volleyball (as measured by Google Trends) is a strong negative predictor of NBA players from that country. Further, this tends to show up in a sharp

---

[16] https://www.facebook.com/officialteamflightbrothers/videos/jericho-sims-hit-his-face-on-the-rim-/490633892042185/

reduction in NBA forwards in volleyball-mad countries. The volleyball-crazed country of Brazil has given the NBA 5 guards and 9 centers – but only 2 forwards. And overall, countries in which volleyball is the most popular produce 75 % fewer NBA forwards.

Why?

The ideal volleyball forward has the same body type as the ideal NBA forward.

So what do you do if you are a 6'9" man who can leap and run fast? In the United States, where basketball is 8 times more popular than volleyball, the decision is a no-brainer. LeBron James, Kevin Durant, and Carmelo Anthony never seriously tried volleyball.

But, in Iran, where volleyball is 5 times more popular than basketball, the decision may feel like a no-brainer in the opposite direction. Volleyball also holds great appeal for men in Poland, Bulgaria, Brazil, Russia, and the numerous other countries where volleyball's popularity tops that of basketball.

By the way, it seems that many tall, high-flying volleyball players made a mistake in picking the sport to specialize in – at least from a financial perspective.

Kaziyski is one of the highest-paid volleyball players in the world; Trentino Volley pays him an estimated 300,000 Euro salary ... which is some 3 times lower than the minimum salary in the NBA. For comparison, the aforementioned Jericho Sims, an awful shooter who can't do a whole lot more than leap within 3 inches of Kaziyski, will earn a guaranteed $1.93 million from the New York Knicks in 2023-2024.

Volleyball requires many of the same skills as being a forward in basketball. But it doesn't quite pay like basketball does.

Chapter 3: The Basketball Genes

The movie *The Pursuit of Happyness* focuses on the relationship between a four-year-old boy and his single dad, a struggling entrepreneur played by Will Smith.

One misty Saturday morning, the father takes his young son to play basketball on an elevated court surrounded by a chain-link fence. The son, wearing a half-zipped blue hoodie and an afro, heaves the ball from behind his shoulders towards the basket. As the ball swishes through the net, the young boy exclaims, "Hey dad, I'm going pro! I'm going pro!"

His father giggles. He takes the basketball into his hand, examines it for a few seconds, and shoots it himself, accidentally throwing the ball above the rusting backboard. The father tells his son:

> *"I don't know. Ya know, you'll probably be about as good as I was. That's kinda the way it works, ya know? And I was below average. So you'll probably ultimately rank somewhere around there. So really, you'll excel at a lot of things. Just not this. So I don't want you out here shooting this ball around all day and night."*

The son is crushed. He throws his basketball away in anger. Then he walks, with his head down, towards the fence, to retrieve his ball and shove it in a plastic bag.

As soft music plays, the father sees his dejected son. He walks towards his son, puts his hand on the fence, stares at the gray sky and, then, lovingly, at his boy. The father changes his verse. He now tells his son:

> *"Don't ever let somebody tell you you can't do something. Not even me. Alright? You got a dream. You gotta protect it. People who can't do something themselves. They want to tell you you can't do it. You want something. Go get it. Period."*

Father and son walk home together.

People love this scene. I mean, people really, really, love this scene. On YouTube, it has more than one million views and thousands of likes. Commenters call it "inspiring," "one of my favorite scenes of all time," and "advice I'm giving my future child."

How could you not be moved by the father's obvious love for his son? How could you not be inspired by his advice -- that his son should follow his dreams? How could you not want to give similar, heart-warming counsel to your own children, to tell them they can do anything they dream of, anything at all?

You would have to be some kind of monster to have a different response to this scene.

Dear reader, I am that monster.

In this chapter, I am going to argue that kids without the right genetic advantages have close to zero chance of becoming great basketball players, as basketball talent is hugely genetically determined. And the evidence, as I have written previously, all comes down to twins.

***

If being good at a skill relies heavily on one's genetics, we should see an unusual number of identical twins at the top of that field.

Why? Because identical twins share 100 % of genes. So, if one person just happens to get a great draw of genetics, his identical twin brother would get that same draw of genetics. (You shouldn't see quite the same concentration of fraternal twins or non-twin brothers, who only share, on average, half their genes.)

Here are the numerous identical twins who have reached the NBA:

The Twins of the NBA

	Twins	Type
1	Dick and Tom Van Arsdale	Identical
2	Horace and Harvey Grant	Identical
3	Carl and Charles Thomas	Identical
4	Jarron and Jason Collins	Identical
5	Joey and Stephen Graham	Possibly Identical
6	Brook and Robin Lopez	Identical
7	Marcus and Markieff Morris	Identical
8	Travis and David Wear	Identical
9	Aaron and Andrew Harrison	Identical
10	Caleb and Cody Martin	Identical
11	Amen and Ausar Thompson	Identical

Indeed, I have estimated that an identical twin of an NBA player likely has a greater than 50% chance of becoming an NBA player himself.[17]

---

[17] As there are not comprehensive records of all brothers of NBA players, for this exercise, I had to assume that parents of NBA players have identical twins at an average rate.

How does the prevalence of identical twins in basketball compare to other sports? I looked at data from the top performers in a wide range of sports.

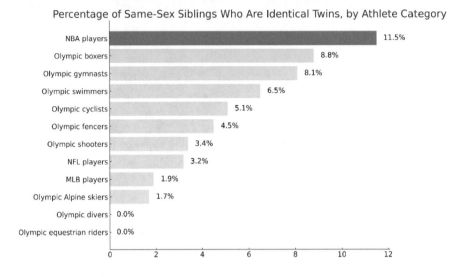

Percentage of Same-Sex Siblings Who Are Identical Twins, by Athlete Category

Athlete Category	Percentage
NBA players	11.5%
Olympic boxers	8.8%
Olympic gymnasts	8.1%
Olympic swimmers	6.5%
Olympic cyclists	5.1%
Olympic fencers	4.5%
Olympic shooters	3.4%
NFL players	3.2%
MLB players	1.9%
Olympic Alpine skiers	1.7%
Olympic divers	0.0%
Olympic equestrian riders	0.0%

Note that the dominance of identical twins in basketball far exceeds that of many other sports – such as football and baseball. This is a dead giveaway that basketball skill is more dependent on genetics than other sports.

So, just how much do genetics contribute to basketball skill? It turns out, you can build a model similar to the one that scientists of genetics do to estimate the contribution of nature and nurture to athletic skill. I estimated the contributions of nature and nurture that were most likely to lead to the prevalence of identical twins and other siblings that we see in the NBA – and in other sports.[18]

---

[18] More details can be found in the mathematical appendix.

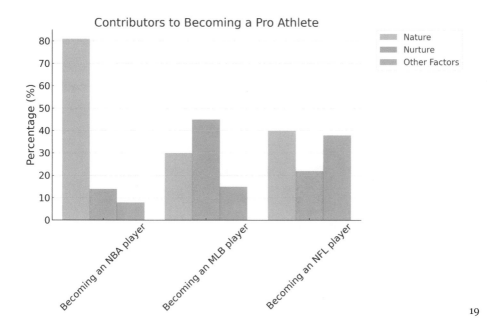

Contributors to Becoming a Pro Athlete

[19]

Basketball, the data from the enormous prevalence of identical twins implies, is more than 80 percent genetic. Basketball has about twice as high a reliance on genetics as football or baseball.

Why are genetics so important in basketball?

A big reason that basketball is so genetic is the importance of height, which was the theme of a previous chapter. Height has a large genetic component (about 80%.)

However, even non-height basketball skills have a substantial genetic component. I looked for every paper I could find that estimated the genetic contribution for a variety of skills – and averaged them. The preliminary results are in the chart that follows.

---

[19] In this chart, you can think of nature as genetics; nurture as anything related to where someone grows up; and other factors referring to anything else, including luck or random decisions over the course of a life.

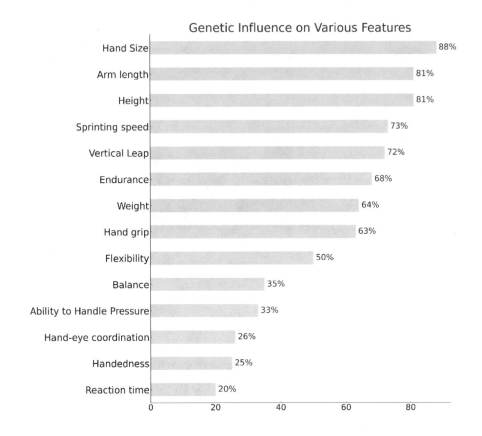

Genetic Influence on Various Features

Feature	Percentage
Hand Size	88%
Arm length	81%
Height	81%
Sprinting speed	73%
Vertical Leap	72%
Endurance	68%
Weight	64%
Hand grip	63%
Flexibility	50%
Balance	35%
Ability to Handle Pressure	33%
Hand-eye coordination	26%
Handedness	25%
Reaction time	20%

Arm length, hand size (which is crucial for reasons we will discuss in a later chapter), and vertical leap are all traits that are more than 70 % genetic. Basketball feels like a sport that was designed in a lab to maximize its reliance on things that can only be achieved through the right DNA.

Other sports where the most important skills might be reaction times, hand-eye coordination, balance, or flexibility will have a lower genetic component than basketball. As I have advised in a previous book, *Don't Trust Your Gut*, if you aren't given extraordinary genetic athletic traits, consider choosing something other than basketball. Perhaps try diving, equestrian riding, or skiing, which you might have a better shot at – even if salaries aren't quite as large.

Chapter 4: Like Father, Like (Better-Shooting) Son

When Kobe Bryant was a kid, he would mop the sweat off the floor of the courts his dad played on. When Steph Curry was a kid, he would take warmups alongside the Charlotte Hornets players. When Jalen Brunson was a toddler, he was spending so much time around adult NBA players, including Larry Johnson and Marcus Camby, that his mom enrolled him in pre-K so he could meet kids his own age. When Klay Thompson was a kid, he would play two-on-two backyard games organized by his NBA-playing father. In the summer, he would hone his skills against Kevin Love, another son of an NBA player. Kobe Bryant, Steph Curry, Jalen Brunson, Klay Thompson, and Kevin Love are among the 103 NBA players who had fathers who also played in the NBA.[20]

How much of an edge does having an NBA father give an aspiring NBA player?

We can calculate the odds of an average American boy reaching the NBA: roughly 1 in 32,000. And we can also calculate the odds of an average son of an NBA player: roughly 1 in 43.[21] This means that having an NBA player as a father increases someone's odds of making the NBA by a factor of 744 – or 74,300%.

This is an astronomical advantage. But the edge fathers pass to their sons in the NBA is actually significantly lower than

---

[20] Kobe Bryant's dad, Joe, was the 14th overall pick in the 1975 draft and played 8 seasons in the NBA. Steph Curry's dad, Dell, retired as the Charlotte Hornets' all-time leader in points and three-point field goals. Jalen Brunson's dad, Rick, played nine seasons in the NBA and has worked for many years as an assistant coach. Klay Thompson's dad, Mychal, was the #1 overall pick in the 1978 draft and averaged 13.7 points and 7.4 rebounds per game in his NBA career. Kevin Love's dad, Stan, was the 9th overall pick in the 1971 draft and played 4 seasons in the NBA before working as a bodyguard, trainer, and assistant to the Beach Boys, a band that featured his brother and cousin.

[21] For these calculations, since I don't know all the sons of NBA players, I assume that NBA players reproduce at an average rate and have males at an average rate. These assumptions may be off by a bit, but the order of magnitude should be right.

the edge fathers pass to their sons in many other glamorous pursuits.

I did the same calculation – comparing the odds of achieving something for an average person and the son of someone who had already achieved it – for a wide range of fields. The edge given to a son has been highest for president, although this is only driven by two people, John Quincy Adams and George W. Bush.

It is also high for billionaires (such as Sam Walton and Bill Walton); reality tv stars (who, like Hulk and Nick Hogan, frequently star in the same show); and Grammy Award winners (such as Bob and Jakob Dylan).

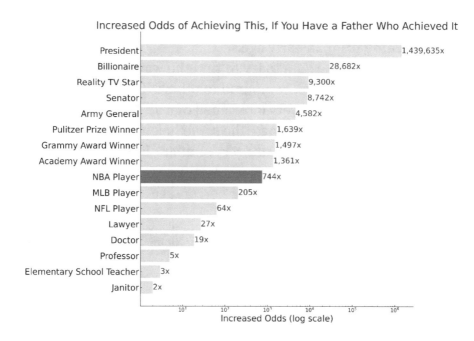

Increased Odds of Achieving This, If You Have a Father Who Achieved It

Field	Increased Odds
President	1,439,635x
Billionaire	28,682x
Reality TV Star	9,300x
Senator	8,742x
Army General	4,582x
Pulitzer Prize Winner	1,639x
Grammy Award Winner	1,497x
Academy Award Winner	1,361x
NBA Player	744x
MLB Player	205x
NFL Player	64x
Lawyer	27x
Doctor	19x
Professor	5x
Elementary School Teacher	3x
Janitor	2x

Increased Odds (log scale)

The reason the NBA and other sports' father-son advantage are lower than some other fields is that sports are legitimate meritocracies, with your performance easy to evaluate.

Billionaires can give their money to their son; reality TV stars can make their show a family affair; senators and Grammy-Award winning artists can give their contacts, which are far more important in fields in which objective ability is harder to judge.

An NBA player can't pass his roster spot to his son or hide the clear poor performance of a son. If you do not play well, you will be cut, even if the team is the New York Knicks and your name is Patrick Ewing Jr.

But, if NBA-playing fathers can't offer enough nepotism to keep their sons on an NBA roster even if they underperform, they do offer two major advantages to their sons.

The first advantage, discussed in the previous chapter, is genetics. And the greatly elevated role of genetics in basketball talent is the reason that the NBA has so much of a larger advantage for sons of players than other sports. That said, even controlling for genetics, sons of NBA players are significantly more likely to reach the NBA than other men.

The second advantage that NBA players offer their sons is good coaching from an early age.

I looked at the data to try to find the ways sons of NBA players are most unique, compared to other NBA players. Mostly, sons of NBA players look a hell of a lot like other NBA players. They have, on average, the same heights and the same weights. Most of their stats are very similar. But there are some differences. The single, most notable difference I could find was ... (drum roll) free throw shooting percentage.

	NBA Players w/ NBA-Playing Fathers	Other NBA Players
Average Height	6'6"	6'6"
Average Weight	209 lbs	209 lbs
Average FT %	75 %	70 %

Sons of NBA players shoot free throws, on average, 5 percentage points higher than other NBA players.[22] [23] And sons

---

[22] The relevant free throw percentages would be 80 percent (for sons of NBA players) and 75 percent (for other NBA players) if the numbers were weighted by free throws attempted, since better shooters tend to attempt more free throws.

[23] Sons of NBA players remain roughly 5 percentage points better free throw

of NBA players are massively overrepresented among the best free throw shooters of all time. Although they only make up about 2 % of all NBA players, players' kids make up 8 % of the top 50 free throw shooters of all time, including the very best free throw shooter, Steph Curry.

A statistically significant percentage of sons of NBA players shoot free throws at a higher clip than their fathers.

These include:

- Jalen Brunson, whose 81.2 % is better than his dad Rick's 69.3 %.
- Cole Anthony, whose 86.1 % is better than his dad Greg's 73.3 %.
- Gary Trent Jr., whose 82.7 % is better than his dad Gary's 64.3 %.
- Kobe Bryant, whose 83.7 % is better than his dad Joe's 74.3 %.
- Klay Thompson, whose 85.2 % is better than his dad Mychal's 65.5 %.
- Rex Chapman, whose 80 % is better than his dad Wayne's 69.1 %.
- Steph Curry, whose 90.9 % is better than his dad Dell's 84.3 %.

Why are sons of NBA players so much better free throw shooters?

In his brilliant book *Range*, David Epstein asks whether it is better to specialize early or come to a pursuit late. He argues, marshaling a wide range of academic evidence, that the surprising answer, frequently, is late. Many of the world's highest achievers sampled many options, learned a wide variety of skills, and finally put them to use on their eventual craft at an older age than their peers. Often, people who come late to a

---

shooters when controlling for year they started their career.

game play the game in a special way that was only allowed by the other skills that they had mastered. Think, for example, of Nikola Jokić. Jokić did not specialize in basketball until his teenage years; in his younger years, he focused predominantly on water polo. His water polo experience, no doubt, helps him in seeing the entire court and passing. As the *New York Times* has put it, "Nikola Jokic Plays Basketball as if It's Water Polo."

That said, there can be an advantage to early specialization in what Epstein refers to as a "kind" environment. A "kind" environment, Epstein explains, is "one where patterns recur, ideally a situation is constrained – so a chessboard with very rigid rules and a literal board is very constrained – and importantly, every time you do something you get feedback that is totally obvious, all the information is available, the feedback is quick, and it is 100% accurate. And this is chess, and this is golf: you do something, all the information is available, you see the consequences, the consequences are completely immediate and accurate, and you adjust accordingly."

Free throw shooting is about as kind an environment as you can get. And, in kind environments, the way to succeed is to start as early as possible with correct feedback on how to improve.

Sons of NBA players usually start playing basketball from a very young age. And their shooting form is taught to them by men who spent years getting the best coaching on shooting form.

"He always shot with the perfect form," former NBA player Melvin Booker has said of his son Devin, the 36th best free throw shooter of all time. "Seeing it, I would never let him shoot another way but the correct way regardless whether he was shooting on a big basket or a small basket, big ball, small ball, whatever. He was always shooting with correct form."

My favorite example of a son taking advantage of this early coaching to outshine his dad in free throw shooting may be Bol Bol.

Manute Bol grew up tending cattle on his family farm in Sudan and dabbling in soccer. He took up basketball at age 15 when he grew too tall for soccer. However, Manute Bol, with his late start to the game, was a lousy free throw shooter – under 60 %.

Manute Bol passed some, but not all, of his enormous height to his son. (Manute Bol is 7'7"; Bol Bol is 7'2".) But Manute also passed on everything he had learned as a professional basketball player to his son at a young age. Bol Bol, with his dad's encouragement, started playing basketball at the age of 4. Bol Bol massively improved on his dad's free throw shooting – to some 75 %, almost 20 % better than his father and well above average for an NBA center.[24]

---

[24] One dynamic among NBA father-son pairs that we commonly see is the father is a poor shooting Big Man and the son is a great shooting guard. Mychal Thompson was a 6'10" center who shot 66 % from the free throw line. His son, Klay, is a 6'6" shooting guard who is an 85 % free throw shooter. Gary Trent was a 6'8" power forward who shot 64 % from the free throw line. Gary Trent Jr. is a 6'5" shooting guard who shoots 81 % from the free throw line. Again, NBA-playing fathers do not pass on all of their height to their sons, due to regression to the mean. But they pass on their knowledge, which helps their sons become extraordinary shooters.

Chapter 5: Why Have So Many NBA Players Been Named Chris?

The most popular name among Black American NBA players is ... Chris. Among such players born in the 1970s and 1980s, there have been 22 men named Chris. This easily beats the second-place name, James, and third-place name, Marcus. Here's a word cloud of all the first names.

First Names of Black American-Born NBA Players

Why am I telling you this? This seems like merely a piece of trivia, no more than a fun fact that you can share at a cocktail party. But, don't be fooled; it is so much more than that. In this seemingly trivial fact are lessons about some of the most important and complex topics in contemporary American society, including race, class, segregation, opportunity, equality, and success.

Socioeconomics and the NBA

Let's start with a simple question: Who is more likely to make the NBA, a poor kid or a middle-class kid?

For many years, the standard answer to this question was: a poor kid. After all, many argued, a poor boy had more drive, more ambition, more desperation, fewer outside options. In the book *The Last Shot*, Darcy Frey quotes a college coach questioning whether a suburban player was "hungry enough" to compete against kids from the ghetto.

But, in fact, research has shown that coming from a less privileged background has always been a substantial disadvantage in making the NBA. This was first demonstrated in a paper by Joshua Kjerulf Dubrow and Jimi Adams. Closely examining the backgrounds of 155 NBA players, they estimated that a Black man from a lower-class background was 37 percent less likely to become an NBA player. A White man from a lower-class background was 75 percent less likely to become an NBA player.

My own analysis looked at the number of NBA players — White and Black —who hailed from every county in the United States. I found that the most affluent counties produce NBA players at a rate 1.6 to 3 times higher than the least affluent counties.

Likelihood of Reaching the NBA by Socio-Economics of County of Birth

Group	Poorest 20%	Second 20%	Middle 20%	Fourth 20%	Richest 20%
Black Males Who Reach NBA (per 1 million births)	42	31	37	63	67
White Males Who Reach NBA (per 1 million births)	1	1	2	3	3

I also looked closely at the family backgrounds of NBA players. I found that, compared to the general Black population, Black NBA players are 32 percent less likely to be born to unmarried mothers and 36 percent less likely to be born to a teenage mother. (I didn't have a large enough sample for this study to test White NBA players, as it is estimated that more than 80% of American-born NBA players are African-American.)

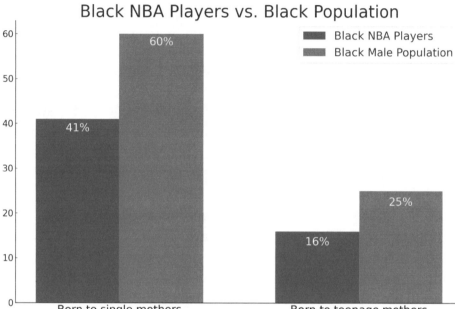

Black NBA Players vs. Black Population

But my favorite clue of the demographics of NBA players comes from their names (hence, the title of this chapter).

A paper by Roland Fryer and Steven Levitt studied naming patterns among Black Americans in the 1990s. They found that 13 percent of Black children are given a unique name – a name that no other kid is given that year. Such names might be Torraye, Etdrick, Uneqqee, or LeBron. And such names are far more likely to be given by unmarried, less educated, and less affluent parents. The rates of unique names are as high as 20 percent in the poorest communities.

I analyzed data on the first names of NBA players. I found that only 7 percent were given unique names, significantly lower than the Black American population, generally. Names among African-American players in the NBA are tilted heavily towards common names, names that are much more likely to be given by those in higher socioeconomic classes.

Want to know the socioeconomics of NBA players? Just listen to games. Chris passing the ball to Mike, trying to get past Brandon and attempting to alley-oop it to Marcus, are the names of the Black middle class, upper middle class, and rich.

The Disadvantages of an Underprivileged Background

Why are boys born to lower socioeconomic status so much less likely to reach the NBA? The first reason relates to the first chapter of this book: height. Due to poorer nutrition, poorer Americans tend to have, according to recent research, stunted adult height.

The second reason may be poorer development of noncognitive skills. Economists have found that one of the major advantages of high socioeconomic status is having the greater opportunity to develop noncognitive skills, such as self-regulation, discipline, interpersonal skills, and trust.

And noncognitive skills are crucial for navigating a team sport such as basketball.

The graveyard of great basketball prospects who never reached the NBA is filled with boys from underprivileged backgrounds whose careers were derailed by not having enough opportunity to develop noncognitive skills. Just consider the heart-wrenching tale of Doug Wrenn, who was rated among the top high school basketball players in the 1990s.

According to his coach, Jim Calhoun at the University of Connecticut, Wrenn jumped the highest of any man he had ever coached. But Wrenn, who was raised by a struggling mother in one of the poorest neighborhoods of Seattle, would taunt players, question coaches, and violate team rules. He was kicked off the University of Connecticut team. He got a second chance at the University of Washington. But, after fighting with coaches, he was kicked off that team as well.

Wrenn was never drafted, moved back in with his mother, and eventually was imprisoned for assault. As he told the *Seattle Times* in 2009, "My career is over. My dreams, my aspirations are over. Doug Wrenn is dead."

Compare Wrenn's story to that of Michael Jordan. Jordan grew up in a middle-class family. His father was an equipment supervisor at General Electric; his mother worked as a banker.

Jordan could, like many super competitive people, at times, have a difficult personality. He was kicked out of school for fighting at the age of 12. But his parents consistently worked on his noncognitive skills. After being kicked out of school one day, Jordan was taken by his mom to her workplace. She forced him to sit in the parking lot reading books. When Jordan first joined the Bulls, his parents and siblings took turns visiting him to help him avoid all the temptations that come with NBA stardom.

Jordan's career, of course, did not end with a little-read quote in the *Seattle Times*. It ended with an induction into the Hall of Fame. In his Hall of Fame speech, Jordan said he tried to stay "focused on the good things about life—you know how people perceive you, how you respect them . . . how you are perceived publicly. Take a pause and think about the things that you do. And that all came from my parents."

The data tells us unambiguously that Jordan is right to thank his middle-class parents. The data tells us that in less privileged families, in less privileged communities, there are NBA-level talents who never reached the NBA. Such men had the talent but may never have been given all the opportunities that help young men fully reach their potential.

What should we make of this analysis? For one thing, we must give that much more credit to any player who came from an underprivileged background. Just as our analysis of the relationship between height and reaching the NBA forces us to give more credit to short players such as Muggsy Bogues, the relationship between socioeconomic status and reaching the NBA forces us to give more credit to players from less affluent backgrounds, such as Jimmy Butler, Kawhi Leonard, and, yes, LeBron James.

After winning his second N.B.A. championship, James was interviewed on television. He said: "I'm LeBron James. From Akron, Ohio. From the inner city. I am not even supposed to be here." Twitter and other social networks erupted with criticism. How could such a supremely gifted person, identified from an absurdly young age as the future of basketball, claim to be an underdog? The more I look at the data, the more it becomes clear that Mr. James's accomplishments are more exceptional than they may appear to be at first. Anyone from a difficult environment, no matter his athletic prowess, has the odds stacked against him.

Interlude: A Humble Ask From The Author

Before continuing, I have an ask. For this book, I have a new, incredibly annoying, commercially-minded publisher (me) who keeps on insisting I monetize this book in a way that will allow me to keep writing them. If you enjoyed *Who Makes the NBA*, I would love it if you left a review on Amazon. I would also love it if you recommended it or gifted it to some friends who you think might enjoy it. Now, back to basketball.

Chapter 6: Who Chokes?

NBA players sometimes attempt pressure shots with millions of people watching.

Can they handle the pressure? Can they deliver in the clutch?

For the average NBA player, the answer is: no.

Or, at least, the average NBA player feels the pressure – and performs worse in clutch moments. The average NBA player shoots free throws 1 percentage point lower in clutch moments – defined by NBA.com as the score within 5 points and fewer than 5 minutes left – than they do in other situations. And the average NBA player shoots free throws 1.5 percentage points lower in clutch moments in playoff games. (In this chapter, I will study free throws because they are controlled experiments, with every shot from the exact same distance with no defender.)

Players vary in how poorly they perform in the clutch. In fact, the average drop in performance in clutch moments is driven by a set of players with dramatically lower clutch free throw percentages than non-clutch free throw percentages. Here are the 34 players with a statistically significant drop in free throw percentage in clutch moments:[25]

_____

[25] Data starts with the 1996-1997 season, when NBA.com starts recording clutch shooting

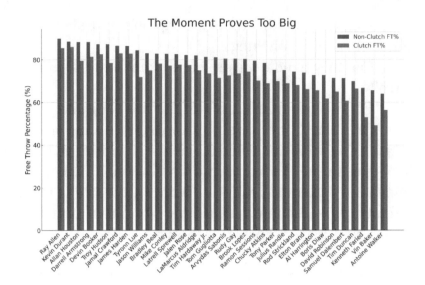

The Moment Proves Too Big

But there are also players who are unaffected by big moments. These are the 30 players who are in the top 200 in total clutch free throws taken and have the smallest difference between their non-clutch and clutch free throw percentage.

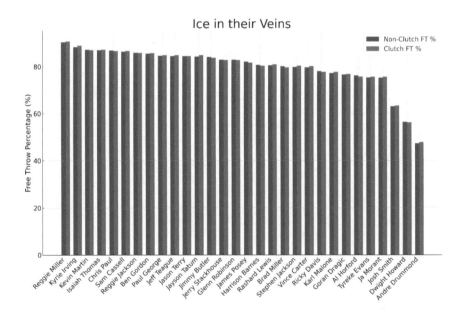

Ice in their Veins

By the way, there is little evidence that any player is capable of improving their performance in the clutch.[26] NBA players are divided between those who remain the same under pressure and those who get worse.

Why do some players choke under pressure?

First, a detour on how surprising this is. In baseball, the game in which data has been pored over the most, it has consistently been shown there is no difference in how professional players perform in the clutch. The average Major League Baseball player is just as likely to make a good pitch or get a base hit in the least consequential points in the game and the most consequential points in the game.

The explanation for this is that, if you weren't mentally tough enough to handle pressure situations, you wouldn't make it to the Major Leagues.[27] Players for whom the big moment proves too big have their baseball careers ended by poor clutch performance long before they are playing on baseball's biggest stage.

But, in basketball, the data shows, this is not the case. Many players – from Arvydas Sabonis to Brook Lopez to Vin Baker – struggle to handle pressure. These NBA players, quite simply, have a tendency to choke.

Why?

I tested a lot of theories on what makes someone worse under pressure.

I thought players who were poor performers in the clutch may not have enough practice in clutch moments. Perhaps Chris Paul is a better clutch shooter than others because he has taken more than 700 free throws in his life. It turns out there is no significant relationship between how many times players have

---

[26] There is only one player in the dataset who has a statistically significant higher free throw percentage: Shane Battier. However, we might expect one player to have a statistically significant higher percentage just by chance.

[27] In a book in which I analyze the clutch ability of players from the comfort of my living room, I should admit that my baseball "career" was limited by an inability to perform in the clutch, among severe athletic shortcomings.

attempted clutch free throws and their tendency to choke. Nor do players tend to become better clutch shooters over the course of their careers.[28]

I thought players might become comfortable in the clutch because they hit some big clutch shots that gave them confidence. But, it turns out, there is no improvement in clutch performance after hitting a buzzer-beating shot. A player is just as likely to choke in the games immediately after he makes a buzzer-beating shot.

I thought players who had experienced more adversity in childhood might perform better in the clutch. Jimmy Butler, who is a legendary clutch performer, had a notoriously challenging upbringing. His father abandoned the family and his mother kicked him out of the house, telling him, "I don't like the look of you." Such upbringing, I surmised, might toughen someone. How much pressure can a free throw be when you've been through all that? But, it turns out, there is no relationship – positive or negative – between the challenges one went through during childhood and one's tendency to choke.[29]

I was close to giving up on understanding why some NBA players choke – and cutting this chapter from my book – until I remembered the variable that keeps coming up in understanding the game of basketball: height.

Height, it turns out, is a significant predictor of tendency to choke – the only variable I could find that predicts it. Yes, taller players, on average, are worse free-throw shooters, as discussed in Chapter 1. But taller players also experience a much larger dropoff in free-throw shooting in clutch moments.

---

[28] The average player increases his free throw percentage by about 0.1 percentage points each year of his career. He increases his clutch free throw percentage by roughly the same amount. Thus, the difference remains constant throughout his career.

[29] There is also no correlation among brothers in the NBA and tendency to choke, suggesting genetics do not play a major role. This fits a lot of research suggesting nature and nurture play a small role in one's ability to handle stress, and other factors play the predominant role.

By this reckoning, taller players, on average, deal with pressure worse than shorter players.[30] In fact, the average 6-foot NBA player shoots clutch free throws at the exact same rate as they shoot non-clutch free throws. But, as players get taller, their clutch free throw percentage drops. The average 7-foot player shoots clutch free throws 6.3 percentage points worse than they shoot non-clutch free throws.

Why is height so correlated with choking?

This relates again to the theme of the first chapter, on just how big an advantage height is in reaching the NBA. Because one in seven 7-footers reach the NBA, very tall players do not go through a ruthless selection process.

What is true among Major League Baseball players of all heights or relatively short NBA players – that they have to be extraordinary at all core skills; otherwise, they get weeded out before reaching the highest levels of the sport – just isn't true for very tall basketball players. Thus, very tall NBA players – even very tall Hall of Fame NBA players – can be surprisingly slow, surprisingly poor jumpers, and surprisingly bad free throw shooters. And, now, we can add, they can also be surprisingly bad at handling pressure.

In fact, I will now update the chart from the first chapter on how much worse athletes tall NBA players are than short NBA players to incorporate this new piece of data on tall players' tendency to choke.

---

[30] Of course, as can be seen in the "Ice in Their Veins" chart, there are many tall players who are great clutch shooters, including Karl Malone, Brad Miller, and Dwight Howard. The worse performance of tall players on various traits merely represent averages. There are great-leaping 7-footers, great shooting 7-footers, extremely fast 7 footers, and clutch 7-footers.

Tall NBA Players Are Way Worse Athletes Than Short NBA Players

	Avg <=6 foot NBA Player	Avg >=7 foot NBA Player
Time to Sprint ¾ Court	3.18 secs	3.54 secs
Vertical Leap	37.5 in.	29.3 in.
Bench Press (185 lbs)	8.6 reps	7.0 reps
Body Fat	6.1 %	8.1 %
Free Throw Shooting	73.9 %	63.1 %
Three Point Shooting	29.4 %	16.5 %
Clutch Free Throw Shooting	Same as Non-Clutch	6.3 pp Worse Than Non-Clutch

A Modest (Not Particularly Serious) Proposal to Fundamentally Change the Game of Basketball

I do not mean to belabor this point. And I know I have talked a lot already about the difference between short NBA players – who are always uber-elite athletes – and tall NBA players – who frequently are not. But this clutch analysis really was the final straw for me. I began to wonder if basketball would be a better league if there were a height cutoff.

Think about it. Because extreme height proves so valuable and so rare, we allow a shocking level of poor play and ineptitude from the tallest NBA players.

The tallest NBA players tend to not be particularly good at one of the core abilities of basketball: shooting. Some of them, such as Hall of Famer Ben Wallace (6'9") and All Star DeAndre Jordan (6'11"), shoot free throws below 50 %.

The tallest NBA players often don't even like basketball. James Harden said that "most players don't really love basketball. They just do it because ...they're tall." Two-time MVP Nikola Jokić (6'11") has famously talked about not particularly liking the job of being a professional basketball player. He describes basketball as "something that I'm good at."

The tallest NBA players sometimes may not need to work as hard as the shorter ones. Phil Jackson said that Shaquille O'Neal (7'1") could have won 10 consecutive MVP Awards if he just worked harder. O'Neal admitted there was some truth to this and that he never worked hard in practice.

And the tallest NBA players often choke in big moments. Vin Baker (6'11") shot 16.4 percentage points worse in clutch moments than non-clutch moments. This is the type of choking that just isn't allowed in other sports.

In the NBA, because having a guy on the court who is among the tallest people in the world proves such an advantage, we are watching games with many players who may not care about the sport, may not work that hard, may lack fundamental skills, and may perform far worse in the most exciting moments.

I love basketball (obviously), and find it one of the most beautiful games on the planet. But could it even be more beautiful?

What would happen if we had a height limit? (Just to be clear, I'm not actually advocating for limits of any sort but just wanted to see what potential impact it might have. Some of my favorite basketball players of all time, including my childhood idol Patrick Ewing, have been 7-footers.)

As an intellectual exercise, I simulated the effects of height limits on the average basketball ability of NBA players. If the height limit were too low, we would miss out on many great basketball talents. But if we added a height limit and it was too high, we would still have many people who were getting by just on their height.

It turns out the height limit that maximizes the basketball talent of NBA players would be 6'0".

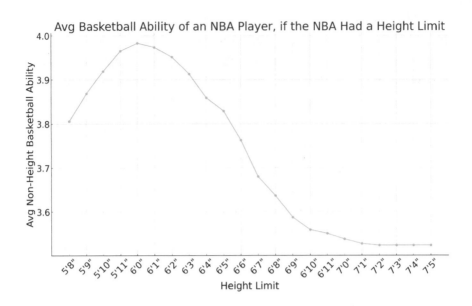

Avg Basketball Ability of an NBA Player, if the NBA Had a Height Limit

If the NBA had a height limit of 6'0", there would be more amazing shooters, world-class leapers, and players with the ability to withstand enormous pressure. Of course, this is not because there is anything fundamentally wrong with the intellectual, social, emotional, or athletic makeup of 7-foot men. It is just that, since 5'10" is the average height of an American male, an NBA with a 6'0" height cutoff would be selecting their centers from a pool of millions of men, not dozens of men.

And, with that, I promise you, I am done talking about the limitations of taller NBA players. I am moving on to other topics, starting with the value (or lack thereof) of attending college.

Chapter 7: What Do Warren Buffett and Paul Millsap Have in Common?

In 1947, Warren Buffett, who had been obsessed with business since he was a child, was offered a spot at one of the greatest business institutions in the history of the world, the Wharton School at the University of Pennsylvania.

And, two years later, Buffett left. He transferred to the University of Nebraska after concluding that Wharton was too expensive; he didn't like Philadelphia; and the library at Nebraska was just as good.

Does it matter where you go to college? First, we will talk about the real world. Then, we will talk about basketball.

Clearly, in the real world, there is a *correlation* between the college you attend and various life outcomes. For example, the average Harvard grad makes $123,000, whereas the average Penn State grad earns $87,000. Fully 20 percent of United States Senators attended one of 12 universities – the Ivy League plus Stanford, MIT, Duke, and Chicago.

But do the elite colleges *cause* these elite outcomes? Perhaps the reason that people who attend Harvard and other elite schools earn more money is because of the people who are accepted to Harvard and other elite schools in the first place: people with extraordinary levels of intelligence and work ethic.

In a path-breaking study, Alan Krueger and Stacy Dale attempted to answer this question. They didn't just compare all students who went to, say, Harvard and Penn State. Instead, they looked at students who got accepted to the same schools – but chose different ones. They found – and this was quite shocking – that there was no difference in earnings outcomes.

A recent study led by Raj Chetty used even better data – and found more subtle causal effects of elite colleges. The team looked at people who were on the waitlist to get into an elite university and compared those who got off the waitlist – and were allowed in – and those that were not.

They found that going to an elite undergraduate university doubles your chances of attending an elite graduate school and triples your chances of working for a prestigious firm. However, in the long-run, they found that attending an elite undergraduate institution does not increase your average earnings.

My reading of the evidence is as follows: Elite universities give you a shiny gloss that might help you get an early top job – or to attend another elite institution. But, in the long run, your success is driven by your talent, not where you went to school. And the best schools don't seem to do a whole lot of making you better.

Which brings us back to the theme of this book: basketball.

Does it matter where a basketball player attends college?

The upper echelons of basketball, like the upper echelons of American society, are dominated by people who went to a select few colleges. In fact, more than 20 percent of NBA players went to one of 12 colleges – as seen in the chart that follows.

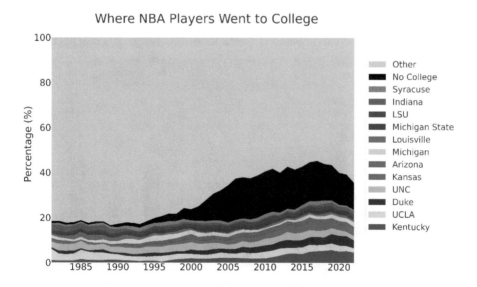

Where NBA Players Went to College

A player who goes to one of these elite basketball schools has a much higher chance of becoming an NBA player than someone who went to a lesser-ranked basketball school. For example, a player who goes to Kentucky has a 55 times higher chance of becoming an NBA player than an average college player.

But is this effect causal? Does going to Kentucky – or to one of the other basketball powerhouses – make a basketball player better? Or are basketball players who go to one of these schools more likely to reach the NBA because these schools attract the best players?

We do have a reasonably objective measure of players' expected talent before attending a college: their recruit rank out of high school. We can compare recruits who were similarly ranked out of high school – but chose to attend differently ranked basketball programs.

And we see a very clear pattern: lower-ranked recruits who attend an elite basketball program are far more likely to reach the NBA. Part of this may be due to better scouting. But part of this appears also due to elite basketball programs doing better at getting their players drafted.

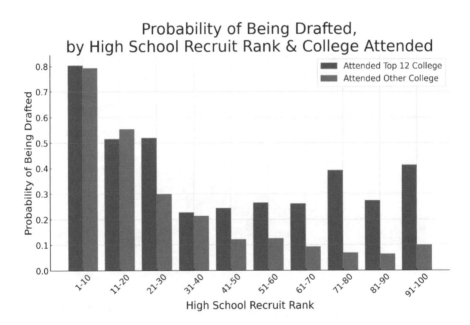

As can be seen, a recruit ranked from 50-100 has a 3-4 times higher chance of reaching the NBA if he attends an elite basketball college. It does seem like these elite basketball programs do help lower-ranked recruits get a shot in the NBA.

But there is a twist.

I also looked at how similarly-ranked recruits who attended different colleges performed in the NBA. I found that, while attending an elite university does help lower-ranked recruits get a shot in the NBA, it does not help them become great NBA players. A lower-ranked recruit who goes to a less-elite school is just as likely to become an NBA All-Star as one who goes to an elite school. In other words, a lower-ranked recruit who does not attend an elite school is more likely to be ignored in the NBA draft. But he is just as likely to turn into a great NBA player, to eventually prove his true worth.

Basketball works just like the real world. Going to an elite school gives a shine that may help you early in your career. But they don't cause you to become better. And, in the long-run, your talent will determine just how high you rise.

And, just as Warren Buffett was able to prove himself as a University of Nebraska graduate, many NBA players prove themselves despite less prestigious basketball degrees. Consider Paul Millsap. Millsap was recruited by Arizona, LSU, and other top programs. He decided to play at Louisiana Tech because he wanted to be really "close to my family." Millsap was drafted in the second round but has massively overperformed his draft spot.

Buffett got rejected from the MBA program at Harvard Business School, perhaps because they were underwhelmed by his Nebraska education. Millsap fell far in the draft, perhaps because teams were underwhelmed by his Louisiana Tech pedigree. But eventually their true talent won out.

Chapter 8: Can You Beat the Draft?

I should be running the New York Knicks' draft. And it is a cruel and unnecessary punishment against little young adorable naive and completely innocent New York basketball fan boys and girls, such as my nephew, Jonah, a budding Knicks fan – that James Dolan has not asked me to. That can be rectified by Googling my email address and offering me the job, which should be done el pronto. Do it for Jonah! That is the important takeaway from this chapter.

Let's start with a fun chart that was created in about 2 minutes with ChatGPT. It shows every draft pick since 1989 and how many win shares they added to their team per season in the NBA. (Win shares is an advanced statistic that attempts to translate a player's stats into how many additional wins the team had because of him. There are other advanced stats, as well; the results in this chapter are very similar using them instead.)

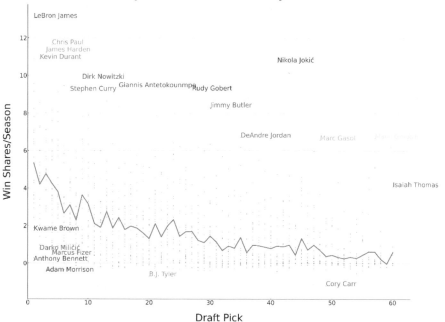

The chart shows, not surprisingly, that there is a strong relationship between draft pick and performance. Generally, players picked earlier perform better.

But there are plenty of outliers; some players drafted in the top few picks, including Adam Morrison and Anthony Bennett, produced very little. Some players drafted in the second round, such as Manu Ginóbili and Isaiah Thomas, became great players.

This chart raises a fundamental question. Can you beat the draft? Can you consistently predict which players will outperform their draft pick?

You could imagine that the answer would be no. You might have a theory – call it the Efficient Draft Hypothesis – that all public information about what makes a good player would be incorporated by teams drafting. Sure, some team might draft a Jokić or a Ginóbili in the second round. But these teams, the Efficient Draft Hypothesis says, just got lucky.

The Efficient Draft Hypothesis, I can report, is not at all true.

The first piece of evidence against the Efficient Draft Hypothesis is that certain teams consistently beat the draft. Some teams draft far more better-than-their-draft-pick-would-suggest players than would be expected from chance. The 23 players drafted by the San Antonio Spurs in the 2010s averaged 0.75 win shares above what would be expected by their draft pick. Similar great performance was achieved by the 13 players drafted by the Toronto Raptors in the same decade.

On the flip side, the 19 players drafted by the Los Angeles Clippers in the 1990s averaged more than 0.5 win shares per season less than would be expected by their draft position. The Phoenix Suns had a similarly dismal draft performance in the 2010s.

In general, the performance of picks on a given team are far more correlated than you would expect by chance. Some teams have figured out something about what makes a good player that the rest of the NBA doesn't know.

The strongest evidence against the Efficient Draft Hypothesis, however, is that it is possible to find traits of players that are correlated with outperforming their draft pick. Some traits are highly predictive of a player being a great pick – or a bust. Here are 4 groups of players that the data suggests have been systematically undervalued in the draft.

Players With Wide Hands

While it doesn't get the attention of some other traits, it is well-known by basketball aficionados that big hands, which allow players to easily palm the ball, are helpful on a basketball court. When Phil Jackson was asked whether he would rather have Michael Jordan or Kobe Bryant on his team, he went with Michael. The reason? Michael has bigger hands than Kobe. When Kobe was asked what he would change about his game, he said he wished he had bigger hands.

Here are some historical great players with enormous hands.

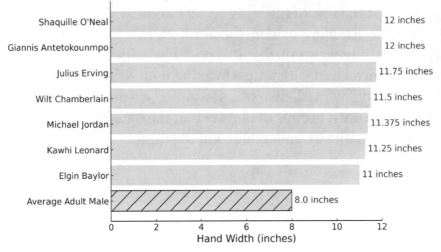

NBA Legends with Legendarily Big Hands

Shaquille O'Neal	12 inches
Giannis Antetokounmpo	12 inches
Julius Erving	11.75 inches
Wilt Chamberlain	11.5 inches
Michael Jordan	11.375 inches
Kawhi Leonard	11.25 inches
Elgin Baylor	11 inches
Average Adult Male	8.0 inches

Hand Width (inches)

But, while it is well-known that hand size is valuable in basketball, it seems that teams have not fully incorporated *just how valuable it is.* I have found that hand width is a significant predictor of players outperforming their draft pick.[31]

---

[31] For this analysis, I first projected the WS/48 that a player could expect based on his draft pick. I then calculated the difference between a player's actual WS/48 and his projected WS/48. Finally, I compared their over or underperformance to their hand width.

Performance Above or Below Expected Draft Spot, by Hand Width

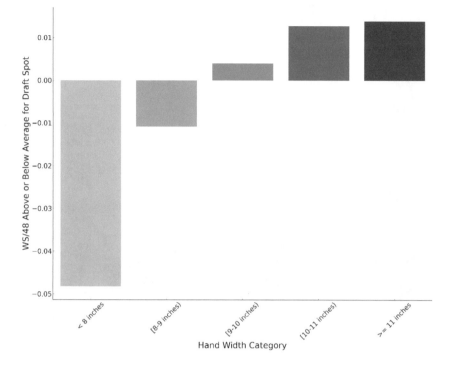

Honestly, I was shocked by the strength of the relationship. There have been 19 NBA players drafted with a hand width of 8.25 inches or less. Seventeen of the 19 players have performed worse than predicted based on their draft spot. And the other 2 only performed about what you'd expect from their draft spot.

You know what they say about men with small hands: they produce far less win shares than their draft spot would predict.

Americans Who Did Not Attend College

One of the most consistent inefficiencies had been undervaluing American men who did not attend college. For a decade-and-a-half – until drafting players out of high school was banned – the straight-from-high-school crowd was massively outperforming their draft position. These include Amar'e Stoudemire (drafted 9th), Kobe Bryant (drafted 13th), Al

Harrington (drafted 25th), Rashard Lewis (drafted 32nd), Lou Williams (drafted 45th), and Amir Johnson (drafted 56th).

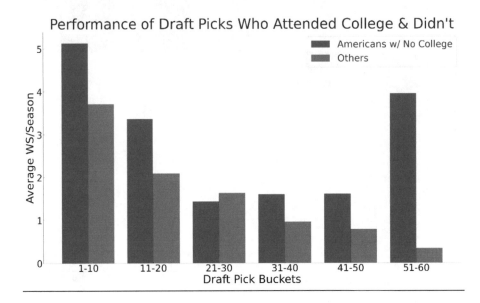

People Who Can Jump High Without a Running Head Start

Here's a question to test your understanding of basketball. Let's say you know 4 things about a player:
1) their height
2) their standing reach (or wingspan)
3) their standing leap (how high they can jump without a running head start)
4) their vertical leap (how high they can jump with a short running head start)

Which 2 are most predictive of how many shots they will block in the NBA?

The answer: standing reach and standing leap.

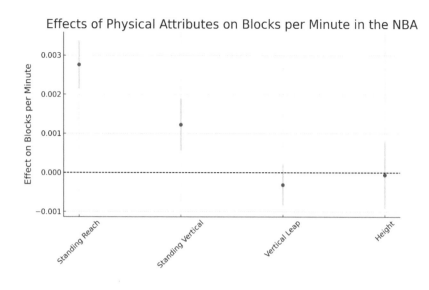

Effects of Physical Attributes on Blocks per Minute in the NBA

Standing reach (or wingspan) is far more important than height. This is because it matters how high you can reach, not how high your head is.

And standing vertical is far more important than vertical leap. This is because, more often than not, in the NBA, you do not get a running head start. While there are some famous examples of blocks in which the player had a full running head start – think of LeBron James' legendary block of Andre Iguodala – most blocks aren't like this. For most blocked shots, you are standing in place and jumping.

It is now common knowledge in the NBA that traditional height is overrated, relative to wingspan. Some people have suggested that statistics-minded teams have used this to their advantage. But my read of the data is that this was long incorporated in the NBA – and players with unusually large wingspans have not been undervalued over the past 20 years.

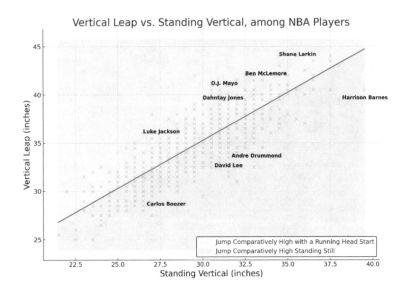

Vertical Leap vs. Standing Vertical, among NBA Players

It is less well-known that standing vertical is more important than vertical leap. For this reason, I have found that players who have a comparatively high standing vertical, relative to their vertical leap – such as David Lee and Harrison Barnes – have been undervalued. Conversely, players who have a comparatively high vertical leap, relative to their standing leap – such as Luke Jackson and O.J. Mayo – have been overvalued.[32]

Teams get confused by the more dramatic running vertical – the people who can leap to the highest possible point. And they forget how often the game of basketball does not require a running head start.

Top-Rated Recruits Who Are Drafted Late

What do Carlos Boozer, DeAndre Jordan, and Trevor Ariza have in common? They were all big-time, top 30 recruits out of high school. They then went to college before being

---

[32] The effect isn't as strong as for some of the other traits in this chapter.

drafted in the second round. And they turned into among the best second-round picks of all time.

This is part of a general pattern. Big-time college recruits who are drafted low massively outperform their draft spot.

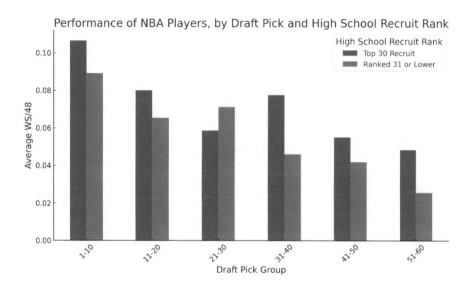

On average, a top 30 recruit is drafted about 8 spots too low in the draft.[33] And a player's recruiting rank in high school is a strongly significant predictor of their overperforming their draft spot.

If the world thinks that a player is a world-class, can't miss prospect and, during college, the world changes its mind, it's probably wise to go with the world's first instinct.

---

[33] The pattern is very similar using different cutoffs for top recruits.

Chapter 9: The Secret of Basketball

"The secret of basketball," Isiah Thomas once told Bill Simmons, "is that it's not about basketball." By this he meant that basketball players get rewarded by scoring points, even if this isn't in the best interest of the team. The secret of basketball, Isaiah thinks, is for players to act in the team's interest, even if it sometimes goes against their own interest.

Is Isiah right? Do players get rewarded too much for taking too many shots and scoring lots of points?

Let's look at the data. I examined how various stats affect a player's contribution to a team's wins; his salary; and his fans on social media.

The Incentives to Be Selfish in Basketball: The Data

First, I measured how various stats contribute to a team's wins. All a player's stats contribute positively to his team's wins. But field goal percentage proves particularly important.[34]

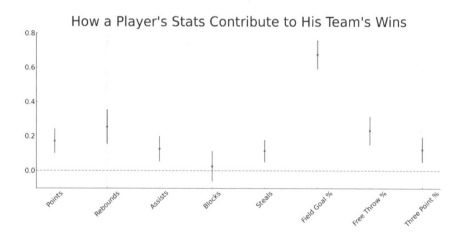

How a Player's Stats Contribute to His Team's Wins

---

[34] This analysis uses WS/48. WS/48 values field goal percentage particularly highly. VORP also shows that all stats contribute positively, but it is less heavily weighted towards field goal percentage.

Next, I measured how various stats contribute to a player's salary.

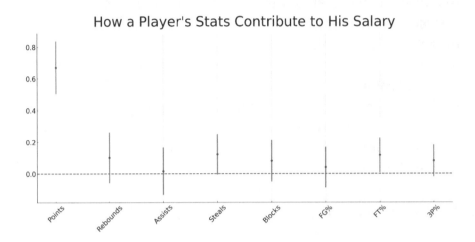

As you can see, the biggest contributor to a player's salary – by far – is how many points he scores. The way to get paid for an NBA player is to score a lot of points. Nothing else will move the needle much, at all.

And here is how a player's stats contribute to his social media fans.

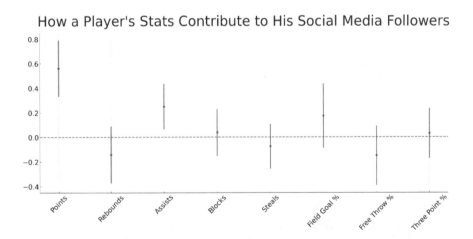

A social media fanbase is almost entirely driven by a player's scoring points – although assists help a bit.

This means that many players who are really good for their teams – because they make a high percent of their shots – don't have as many fans. And many players who have lots of fans may not be particularly good for their teams. They just score a lot of points.

Basketball is indeed a sport with a major incentives problem. Players have a clear incentive to score more points even if it requires taking bad shots, which leads to a higher salary and more fans – and often endorsement deals. But, for a team to win the most games, they need players to not take these bad shots, to instead have a high field goal percentage.

Who, then, can get players to override their incentives?

Chapter 10: On Coaches

How much do coaches matter?

This is one of the most oft-asked questions in basketball – and also one of the most difficult to answer. Clearly, many coaches have enormous success, winning a large percent of their games. Here are the 10 coaches with the highest winning percentage since 1980.

Coaches Since 1980 with Highest Win Percentage

Coach	Win Pct
Billy Cunningham (PHI '80-'85)	72.0 %
Phil Jackson (CHI '89-'98; LAL '99-'11)	70.4 %
K.C. Jones (BOS '83-'88; SEA '90-'92)	69.5 %
Joe Mazzulla (BOS '22-'23)	69.5 %
Larry Bird (IND '97-'00)	68.7 %
David Blatt (CLE '14-'16)	67.5 %
Steve Kerr (GSW '14-'23)	66.5 %
Gregg Popovich (SAS '96-'23)	64.2 %
Pat Riley (LAL '81-'90; NYK '91-'95; MIA '95-'08)	63.5 %
Ime Udoka (BOS '21-'22)	62.2 %

But how much credit do these coaches deserve? After all, just about all these coaches had star players on their teams. Who gets the credit for the Chicago Bulls' success in the 1990s, Michael Jordan or Phil Jackson? Who gets the credit for the Golden State Warriors' success in the 2010s, Steve Kerr or Steph Curry?

The most compelling method that I have come across to measure coaching ability is from Ramzy Al-Amine. Al-Amine attempts to measure the talent on a team based on the stats of players the year before a coach joined the team. I extended Al-Amine's analysis incorporating more information.

I estimate head coaching performance, controlling for talent on the team, as follows:

1. For every player, I estimate the average age-adjusted Win Shares per 48 minutes for seasons in which they were *not* coached by a particular coach.
2. I multiply expected Win Shares per 48 minutes times minutes played and sum up for every team. This finds the Expected Wins, based on the talent of a roster.
3. I subtract Actual Wins-Expected Wins as the value of a coach.

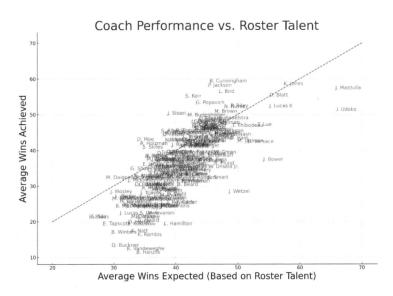

Here is my estimate of the best coaches of the modern era – along with the average wins they add in a given season.

Best Coaches of the Modern Era (Adjusted for Roster Talent)

Coach	Average Wins Added in a Season
Billy Cunningham (PHI '80-'85)	13.5
Steve Kerr (GSW '14-'23)	13.2
Phil Jackson (CHI '89-'98; LAL '99-'11)	12.5
Stan Albeck (SAS '80-83; NJN '83-'84; CHI '85-'86)	11.4
Jerry Sloan (CHI '80-'82; UTA '88-'11)	11.2
Gregg Popovich (SAS '96-'23)	9.6
Larry Bird (IND '97-'00)	9.1
Doug Moe (DEN '80-'90; PHI '92-'93)	8.9
Mike Budenholzer (ATL '13-18; MIL '18-23)	7.5

I do not think this is a perfect measure – and I plan to improve it in the future – but the analysis does suggest that coaches can be extraordinarily important. I am hardly alone in finding this. In fact, this is a growing consensus in the statistical community. Using a variety of methods, math geeks have found that coaches in the NBA have outsized influence. A different study by University of Chicago statisticians Christopher R. Berry and Anthony Fowler found that NBA coaches have more influence on the outcome of games than coaches in any other sport.

How Much Coaches Influence Outcomes

League	Influence (%)
NBA Coaches	31%
NHL Coaches	26%
MLB Coaches	25%
NFL Coaches	21%

Berry and Fowler found that the best NBA coaches can add more than 8 wins per season, which, despite using very different methods, is similar to my estimate.

What, then, do great coaches do?

I tried to find evidence for many theories I had. But many of them proved strikingly difficult to find evidence for.

I thought coaches might make their players hustle more. But any measure of hustle I tested, it didn't show up. I thought coaches might make their players more skilled. But any measure of skill I tested, it didn't show up. I thought the best coaches implement the best systems. But I didn't find much evidence that certain systems are consistently more effective. I thought the best coaches might be better talent scouts and play the best players. But very few teams lose many games due to suboptimal lineups.

I did, however, find one thing that was really significant. Certain coaches get their players to pass more. Here is a ranking of how much various coaches increase (or decrease) players' tendency to pass the ball on a drive to the basket.

Change in How Frequently the Same Player Will Pass on a Drive, When Coached by Them

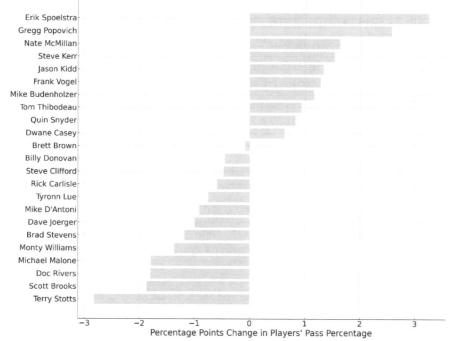

Percentage Points Change in Players' Pass Percentage

And there is evidence that the impact coaches have on their players' passing the ball may go a long way towards explaining their effectiveness. The ability to get players to pass is significantly correlated with my measure of how many wins a coach adds to a team.

I am going to continue to research this, but, based on my preliminary analysis, I suspect that a significant fraction of coaching success can be explained by how much they get players to pass.

This actually makes sense, considering the finding of the previous chapter: the secret of basketball. As Isiah Thomas and others have pointed out – and the data clearly shows – basketball has an incentives problem; players get more money and fans by taking too many shots. The best coaches, then, are able to get players to go against their own self-interest for the betterment of the team.

How do the best coaches do this?

At this point, I gave up on using data to help. But I did come across a possible answer in an excellent book. Daniel Coyle's book *The Culture Code* followed Gregg Popovich, coach for the Spurs, who ranks by any measure as one of the greatest coaches in NBA history – and also is unusually good at getting his players to pass the ball.

Much of what Popovich does, Coyle found, is focused on making the teammates feel connected. The Spurs, Coyle found, spend roughly as much time eating together as they do playing basketball together. They have team dinners and small group dinners, where the discussion is rarely about the Xs and Os. Instead, Popovich leads discussions on politics, war, racism, terrorism, and civil rights.

The message Popovich is trying to get across, in the words of Coyle, is that "there are bigger things than basketball to which we are all connected." The key is seeing the humanity in teammates, seeing them as people, not just players you compete with for points and salary increases. These are the types of conversations that make a player 2.84 percentage points more likely to pass the ball when he is driving to the basket – and that makes the team win 9.6 more games every season.

And Popovich's other secret seems to be: ... (drum roll) ... hugs.

"Hug 'em and hold 'em," Popovich tells his assistant coaches. "We gotta hug 'em and hold 'em."

Yes, readers. To make the NBA, you need it all: enormous size, big hands, a great leap, a wicked shot, great toughness. And, once you are among these select gladiators, to perform to the highest of your ability, you need ... a hug.

Conclusion: What Have We Learned?

When I was a young boy, I had one dream and one dream only: to be an NBA player. Every night, I would play in my room with a ball and a little hoop I'd attached to the wall. I'd imagine the ball was in my hands as the clock ran out. "3-2-1. Seth for the win! Swish!"

If you haven't guessed by now, my dream of reaching the NBA never came to fruition.

To salve my wounds, I have written a book on what it takes to make the NBA – which notes that it is just about impossible for anyone my height to be admitted to this exclusive club.[35]

So what other lessons can we draw from the data?

There are surely lessons in how to pick a career. Robert Plomin, the legendary scientist who studies genetics, recommends that you "go with the genetic flow" in choosing a career. Because genetics play such a big role in ability, pick something for which you have genetic potential.

This is becoming easier as our understanding of genetics improves. Indeed, one academic study has found that Shawn Bradley – the 7'6" former NBA player – had 198 more genetic indicators of potential tallness than the average person. In the future, someone with such genes could be informed of this and, perhaps, begin preparing for a basketball career, maybe by getting basketball coaching at a very young age.

Map my Gene, a company based out of Singapore, offers to test kids' DNA and grade them on 46 talents & traits, including musical ability, sprinting ability, endurance, creativity, drawing, and dancing.

---

[35] Being slow, having a poor vertical leap, and having near-panic attacks during big moments that would inevitably put me on the chokers' list also didn't help.

It is also wise in choosing a career to, in a phrase popular in the business world, "use your unfair advantage." In business school, they teach you, for example, if you have capital, consider starting a business that requires a lot of capital. If you have a social media presence, consider starting a business for which that is an advantage. If your father owns an auto dealership, think about inheriting it.

Even if you don't start a business, you can use whatever unfair advantages you have in whatever you pursue. Consider myself. I was naturally – and unfairly – very good at math. That seems to be largely genetic. My grandmother, who had to stay home to help support the family rather than accept a college scholarship, and my grandfather on the other side, a house painter whose education ended with the Holocaust, both loved and excelled at math puzzles. In addition, my brother is a computer science professor at Cornell.

I also received unfair coaching in writing. My dad was a journalism professor at NYU. Just as Dell Curry has been working on Steph's shooting form since he was a kid, Mitchell Stephens has been working on my writing form since I was a kid.

My most unfair advantages were in math and writing. Hence, I perform data analysis – and write about it.

But the main lesson that I took from writing this book is to chill out about success. Our lives seem to be largely written before we are born.

A lot of rah-rah books preach the value of hard work. *Talent Is Overrated. Discipline Is Destiny.* You can do whatever you set your mind to.

Clearly, for most of us, hard work and discipline alone would not be nearly enough to get us into the NBA – and, if we're going to be honest, hard work and discipline alone are not enough for success in acting, singing, modeling, painting, fiction writing, tech entrepreneurship, and many other pursuits.

Some of the charts in this book can be viewed as depressing. The correlation between parental success and child success. The genetics of success. The correlation between height and success. Here's a (some might argue, depressing) summary of the rigged game that is making the NBA:

Odds of Making it to the NBA, by Various Demographics

Category	Odds
A man born in India	0
A 5'10" American who isn't a son of an NBA player	1 in 900,000
A son of an NBA player	1 in 43
A 7-footer	1 in 7
An identical twin of an NBA player	1 in 2

It is often considered hopeful to tell stories of the possibilities people have to do whatever they want. It is considered a downer to show data – with which this book is filled – showing that many possibilities are off the table.

But I think that is wrong. I view the charts in this book as, in a weird way, uplifting. If you, like me, have a tendency to beat yourself up about all the things that you did not accomplish, it can be freeing to learn that many accomplishments were impossible anyway.

Yes, work hard and be disciplined at something. But remember that a lot of life is out of our control. The place we are born. Our parents. Our height.

Most importantly, enjoy the ride, whether you are an NBA great or merely a guy who watches them play and sometimes gets to write about them.

Appendix 1: Using AI to Create This Book

I have learned a lot about using AI (and particularly ChatGPT and its data analysis tools) in the creation of this book. In this section, I will tell you everything that I have learned which may prove helpful. I have 4 sections:

1) Using AI for Data Analysis
2) Using AI for Writing
3) Using AI for Creating Art
4) Basic & Surprising Lessons About ChatGPT That Can Save You a Lot of Pain.

I will continue to discuss my learnings on Twitter (@SethS_D).

It is important to mention that just about everything I discuss may change over time, as AI's capabilities improve. I am speaking about the current versions of AI, as of 12/8/23.

1) Using AI for Data Analysis

For Collecting Data

In the realm of data collection, ChatGPT offers significant assistance, albeit with some limitations. As of the current version (as of December 8, 2023), ChatGPT does not have the capability to directly access or scrape data from the internet. However, it can be an invaluable tool in processing and analyzing data that you have collected. Here's how you can utilize ChatGPT in your data scraping process:

Manual Data Collection: Begin by visiting the website containing the data you need. Manually save the webpage as an HTML file.

Data Processing with ChatGPT: Once you have your HTML file, open ChatGPT and upload the page. Clearly instruct ChatGPT about the specific data you require from the page. ChatGPT can then assist in extracting and organizing this data from your uploaded file.

This method proved highly effective for projects where datasets were not readily available in an accessible format like .csv. For instance, in a project analyzing the followers of NBA players on Twitter (which was left on the cutting room floor), I manually saved the HTML pages of players' Twitter profiles. Uploading these to ChatGPT and specifying my data requirements allowed me to efficiently gather the necessary information.

While ChatGPT's current version doesn't scrape data directly from the internet, its ability to process and analyze uploaded data files can still save you countless hours in data collection and preparation.

For Merging Data

Merging data is a nuanced and crucial step in data science, fraught with potential complications. It's important to recognize that using ChatGPT for data merging does not diminish the need for vigilance and meticulousness. In fact, overseeing a data merge executed by ChatGPT requires the same level of attention and care as if you were performing the merge manually. The closest I came to really screwing up, relying in ChatGPT, was if I tried to merge a dataset and didn't check it closely.

Key Checks Post-Merge:

Observation Count: Verify if the number of observations after the merge aligns with your expectations. A discrepancy in numbers can signal an issue.

Duplicate Data: Look for unintended duplicates which may distort your analysis. Duplicate entries must be identified and addressed.

Data Integrity: Ensure all pertinent information from the original datasets is retained. Loss of data during the merge can lead to incomplete or skewed results.

Sanity Checks: Plotting key variables from the merged dataset can serve as a sanity check, confirming the logical consistency of your data.

Precision in Instructions:

When instructing ChatGPT to perform a data merge, clarity and precision are paramount. The tool acts on your commands, and any ambiguity can lead to unintended outcomes. Specify the variables for merging, and clearly state whether all observations from each dataset should be retained.

Review and Verification:

Always inspect the code generated by ChatGPT to ensure it matches your intended merging process. Then, closely examine the resulting dataset for accuracy and completeness. Remember, while ChatGPT can automate the process, it cannot replace the critical thinking and scrutiny required in data analysis.

In my experience, challenges with ChatGPT in data merging often stemmed from instructions that weren't precise enough or from not thoroughly reviewing the merge results.

Treating ChatGPT as a tool that requires your guidance and oversight, rather than a fully autonomous solution, is crucial for successful data merging.

Cleaning Data

ChatGPT proves to be a highly effective tool for data cleaning tasks, simplifying what can often be a time-consuming aspect of data analysis. Here are some ways you can leverage ChatGPT for cleaning your data:

Correcting Values: Direct ChatGPT to identify and modify any values in your dataset. For example, you can instruct it to change all negative observations to zero or to change all NA values to 0.

Standardizing Names: Inconsistent naming conventions can lead to errors in analysis. Use ChatGPT to standardize names within your dataset. For instance, instruct ChatGPT to replace any first name that is merely an initial with a full name or remove it, depending on your data requirements.

Uniform Labeling: Ensuring consistent labeling across your dataset is crucial for accurate comparisons and analysis. Command ChatGPT to verify and correct labels. For example, you can have it check that 'University of North Carolina' is uniformly labeled across all datasets, eliminating any variations like 'UNC' or 'North Carolina'.

With clear instructions, ChatGPT can efficiently carry out these data cleaning tasks, significantly reducing the manual effort required and enhancing the overall quality of your data.

Regressions & Summary Statistics

Utilizing ChatGPT for conducting regressions and generating summary statistics can be quite effective and user-friendly. The process is straightforward, akin to guiding a research assistant or intern. When provided with clear and specific instructions, ChatGPT can perform these tasks with a high degree of efficiency and accuracy, much like an ideal research assistant.

However, it's important to note a limitation I encountered in my use of ChatGPT: handling more complex aspects of regressions, such as dealing with standard errors, may not be as robust. While this was not a critical issue for the purposes of this book, it could be a significant consideration for those undertaking more advanced academic research. In academic settings, where the precision of statistical analysis, including standard error calculations, is paramount, this limitation of ChatGPT should be kept in mind.

Therefore, while ChatGPT serves as an excellent tool for basic regression analysis and summary statistics, for more intricate statistical needs, especially in academic research, you might not be able to rely on it.

Ideas and Theoretical Exploration with ChatGPT

One of the most exciting prospects I envisioned with ChatGPT was its potential in aiding the generation of theoretical ideas for research. For example, let's say I wanted to investigate why certain countries produce more or fewer NBA players. The idea was to leverage ChatGPT's extensive knowledge base about these countries. By providing data on countries with the highest and lowest numbers of NBA players, I anticipated that ChatGPT could analyze this information against its vast repository of knowledge on each country. This would ideally allow it to identify shared characteristics or unique factors contributing to this phenomenon.

However, in practice, this approach faced challenges. While ChatGPT possesses a wealth of information on a wide range of topics, including detailed knowledge about various countries, its current capabilities in correlating this extensive knowledge to generate new theories or uncover complex patterns were limited. The tool struggled to effectively synthesize and apply its vast database to create the nuanced insights I was looking for.

This experience suggests that while ChatGPT's extensive knowledge is a powerful asset, the ability to create new theories or deeply analyze correlational data may be enhanced in future versions of the tool. As AI technology continues to advance, it's conceivable that future iterations of ChatGPT will be able to more effectively utilize their expansive databases for sophisticated theory generation and hypothesis exploration.

Optimizing Graphs and Charts with ChatGPT

ChatGPT can be an excellent tool for creating charts and graphs, but it often requires a bit of trial and error to get the perfect output. Here's a method I recommend: initially, ask ChatGPT to generate a chart multiple times, tweaking your request each time until you get a result that aligns with your preferences, especially in terms of aesthetics like color schemes.

Once you find a design that resonates with your taste – for instance, a particular color scheme that stands out – make sure to save the specific code or settings that ChatGPT used to create that design. This becomes your template for future charts.

When you need to create new charts, provide ChatGPT with the saved code or settings as a reference point. This approach ensures consistency in the visual presentation of your charts.

For example, in my project, after several iterations, I developed a preference for a chart design in blue, white, and gray. Once I had this design, I saved the configuration. For subsequent charts, I simply provided ChatGPT with this saved design code, requesting the same style for new data visualizations.

This method not only saves time but also ensures that your charts maintain a consistent and professional look across your work.

Objective Coding of Information with ChatGPT

A notable strength of ChatGPT is its ability to act as an objective coder of information, a feature I found particularly useful in my research. For instance, in my analysis of clutch shooting in basketball, I explored whether there was a correlation between NBA players' childhood background difficulties and their performance in clutch moments. To this end, I utilized ChatGPT to objectively rate the childhood difficulty of each NBA player on a scale from 1 to 10, based on the comprehensive information it has. The ratings provided by ChatGPT were coherent and sensible.

ChatGPT's Ratings of Childhood Difficulty

Player	Rating of Childhood Difficulty	Reason
Allen Iverson	9.0	Grew up in poverty in Hampton, Virginia; mother struggled in a crime-infested environment.
Lamar Odom	8.0	Faced significant challenges. Mother died of colon cancer when he was twelve, raised by his grandmother, as his father was a heroin addict.
Shaquille O'Neal	7.0	Grew up in Newark, New Jersey, in a rough neighborhood; biological father was imprisoned.
Derrick Coleman	6.0	Grew up in a rough neighborhood in Detroit, navigated a challenging environment.
Trevor Ariza	5.0	Faced challenges in Los Angeles, including the impactful loss of his younger brother.
Dwight Howard	4.0	Raised in Atlanta, Georgia, in a religious family; father was a Georgia State Trooper.
Devin Booker	3.0	Son of a professional basketball player, had a supportive environment in Grand Rapids, Michigan.
Steve Nash	2.0	Had a comfortable upbringing in British Columbia, Canada, with family support for his sports endeavors.

Interestingly, childhood background was not correlated with clutch shooting.

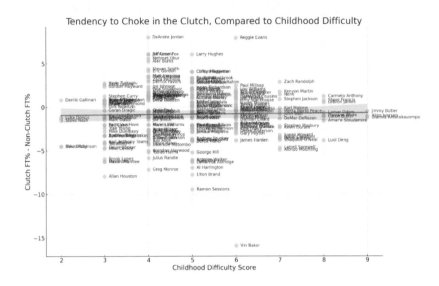

While this (null) result was clear, it highlights a potential ethical concern in using AI for research. Given that ChatGPT can be prompted to reevaluate or recode data, there exists a risk of manipulating the AI's coding process to align with a desired outcome. For example, if I were dissatisfied with the initial lack of correlation, I might be tempted to ask ChatGPT to re-rate the data until a correlation appeared.

This possibility presents a significant dilemma. On one hand, ChatGPT's capability as an objective information coder is invaluable, offering vast potential for various research applications. On the other hand, it introduces a risk of facilitating less-than-honest research practices. This duality necessitates a careful consideration of ethical standards in research when employing AI tools like ChatGPT. It's imperative to use these tools responsibly, ensuring the integrity and honesty of the research remain intact.

2) Using AI for Art

My own journey with art creation for this book was quite enlightening, especially considering my limited interest and proficiency in the field. This experience led me to two key realizations:

The Power of Outsourcing

Despite my lack of artistic expertise, I discovered the effectiveness of outsourcing as a solution. Platforms like Fiverr are treasure troves of talented individuals who are not only skilled in art but also adept at utilizing the latest AI art tools. Engaging with an artist from Fiverr played a crucial role in creating the appealing artwork featured in this book.

Embracing Volume for Quality

A significant lesson I learned was the relationship between quantity and quality in art creation. The art that began the chapter Missing LeBron was the best of about 50 attempts. The process of designing the book cover involved generating hundreds of drafts. This extensive exploration was key in narrowing down to the best options. Further, by engaging multiple artists on Fiverr to work on different versions of the text for the cover and then seeking feedback from a broad audience, I was able to determine the most impactful design.

These insights can be particularly valuable for anyone who feels artistically challenged yet seeks to incorporate quality art into their projects. Leveraging the skills of others and embracing the iterative process of creation can lead to surprisingly impressive results.

3) Using AI for Writing

Assessing ChatGPT's Writing Capabilities

In my experience, ChatGPT's writing ability can be characterized as 'B-level'. It's competent for certain tasks, but may not always meet the needs for more nuanced or unique writing styles. For this book, I opted not to use ChatGPT for the majority of the writing, as I sought a more distinctive voice than what ChatGPT currently offers.

For example, when I requested ChatGPT to rewrite the introduction of my chapter "Missing LeBrons," the output, while coherent and well-structured, came across as overly formal and lacked the engaging tone I desired. It read more like an academic piece than a lively, accessible text.

In conclusion, if 'B-level' writing suffices for your needs, ChatGPT is a viable tool. However, if you're seeking a style that surpasses this level or if you are a more skilled writer, you might find ChatGPT's capabilities limiting.

Enhancing Structure in Writing

Where ChatGPT excels, however, is in structuring and organizing content, especially when initial drafts are rough or hastily written. For instance, in the "Downloading Data" section of my book, my initial draft was somewhat disorganized:

> Scraping data is a total game-changer. As of today, Advanced Data Analysis is not connected to the internet (That is likely to change in the future.) However, you can still use the tool to help with scraping data. The way to do this as follows:

> Go to a website with data that you need. Save the page as an html.
> Open Advanced Data Analytics. Upload the page. And tell Advanced Data Analysis what you need from the page.

This is how I downloaded most datasets that weren't publicly available in a .csv. It likely saved thousands of hours of work.

For one project that didn't make the final book, I wanted to study who NBA players followed on twitter. I went to players' twitter page. And saved their page as an html. I then uploaded that file to ChatGPT and asked it to get me all the followers of the players. And it did it very well.

ChatGPT's restructuring provided a much clearer and logically organized version that you see at the start of this Appendix. In fact, this approach underpinned much of the writing process for this Appendix. I initially laid out my thoughts in a somewhat haphazard manner, and ChatGPT skillfully transformed them into coherent passages. While its writing style might not be exceptionally vibrant or exciting, I found ChatGPT's 'B-level' writing perfectly adequate for the purpose of this Appendix. It efficiently converted my rough ideas into well-structured text, providing clarity and coherence to the content.

Formatting Things Nicely

You should feel comfortable making things fairly sloppy, knowing that ChatGPT will format them. For the Notes section of this book, I wrote things really sloppily, put it in ChatGPT, and asked it to make it look good.

Copy-Editing with ChatGPT

For thorough and reliable copy-editing, ChatGPT emerges as an indispensable tool. Its proficiency in detecting and correcting grammatical errors makes it an excellent resource for refining written work. I have found that inputting an entire chapter into ChatGPT yields highly accurate results, with the AI consistently identifying any grammatical inaccuracies present in the text.

Comparing different iterations of the tool, GPT-4 demonstrates a notable improvement over its predecessor, GPT-3.5, particularly in the realm of grammar checking. While GPT-3.5 had a tendency to incorrectly flag text as having grammatical errors – a phenomenon often referred to as 'hallucinating' errors – GPT-4 shows no such issue. It operates with a higher level of accuracy and, in my experience, has successfully identified every grammatical error in the texts submitted to it.

This enhanced capability makes ChatGPT an invaluable asset in the copy-editing process, ensuring that your chapters, articles, or any written content are not only grammatically sound but also polished and professional.

4) Basic & Surprising Lessons About ChatGPT That Can Save You a Lot of Pain

Managing Session Length with ChatGPT

An important aspect to consider while working with ChatGPT is the management of session length. ChatGPT operates on transformer models that process the entire text within a session, and I've observed that its performance can diminish as the session lengthens. This realization came gradually; in my early experiences, I often engaged in extended, marathon sessions with ChatGPT, only to find the quality of its responses degrading over time, leading to increased errors and less accurate outputs.

To optimize ChatGPT's effectiveness, it's advisable to be mindful of the length of each session. Once you reach a certain threshold – approximately 20 messages, for instance – it's beneficial to save your progress and initiate a new session. This approach helps in maintaining the quality and accuracy of ChatGPT's responses, ensuring more reliable and consistent assistance throughout your project.

Managing Timeouts and Preserving Work in ChatGPT

An important aspect to be aware of while working with ChatGPT is the timeout mechanism. After about 50 messages, ChatGPT enforces a timeout, temporarily restricting further use for a couple of hours. Moreover, when you return to ChatGPT after this break, you'll find that it doesn't retain the details of the previous session. This can render a significant portion of your unsaved work unusable.

Learning to navigate this feature took some time. The key strategy I developed is to consistently save your progress, especially as you approach the message limit. For instance, when working on charts, I created a file named "Working Code to Make Charts in this Book." As I neared the timeout threshold, I would request ChatGPT to provide all the necessary code for the current chart. This code would then be saved in my file. When the timeout period ended, I could simply use this saved code to seamlessly pick up where I left off.

This approach of regular saving and documenting your progress is essential for efficient and uninterrupted work with ChatGPT, ensuring that none of your valuable efforts are lost due to timeouts.

Handling Dataset Sizes with ChatGPT

One factor influencing my decision to focus this book on the NBA, apart from my passion for basketball, was the manageable size of NBA datasets. Most datasets in this realm, including one encompassing every NBA player in history, contain around 4,500 observations. This scale is particularly suitable for the current version of ChatGPT, which tends to encounter memory errors when processing significantly larger datasets.

For larger datasets that exceed ChatGPT's handling capacity, the tool remains useful for assisting in coding. ChatGPT can be employed to develop code tailored to your dataset's analysis needs. However, it's important to note that you'll need to execute this code externally, as ChatGPT is not equipped to run extensive analyses internally due to its memory limitations.

ChatGPT Can Do Things You Might Not Expect; Be Ambitious

The utility of ChatGPT often extends beyond what one might initially expect. It's advisable to continually explore and leverage the full range of ChatGPT's capabilities, as it can often surprise you with what it can achieve.

An example from my experience involves creating a chart detailing the colleges that NBA players attended over time. I challenged ChatGPT with the task of color-coding the chart according to each college's official colors, a task I initially thought might be beyond its capabilities. However, not only did ChatGPT accomplish this, but it also did so impressively.

This experience led me to further utilize ChatGPT's color-coding feature for other charts throughout the book, enhancing their relevance and visual appeal.

Another instance that showcases ChatGPT's capabilities involved the creation of a chart on NBA draft picks. I presented ChatGPT with the challenge of selecting and labeling player names in a way that would not only be engaging but also ensure that the labels didn't overlap, a task requiring both strategic thinking and design acumen. Impressively, ChatGPT successfully executed this task, demonstrating its ability to handle complex visual data representation. This functionality was not only useful but also added a layer of sophisticated analysis and presentation to the chart.

These instances are a testament to the often underappreciated breadth of ChatGPT's abilities. It's worthwhile to experiment and ask ChatGPT to perform tasks even if you're unsure of its capacity to handle them. More often than not, you might find yourself pleasantly surprised by its proficiency and versatility.

Interacting with ChatGPT: A Collaborative Process

Effective use of ChatGPT often resembles an interactive, conversational process rather than a one-off command. It's relatively rare for ChatGPT to deliver the exact desired outcome on the first attempt. The key lies in viewing your interaction with ChatGPT as a dialogue: you ask for something, review the result, and then provide feedback or modifications to refine the output.

Take, for instance, the creation of a backronym for my height-adjusted score of NBA players, which I named 'MUGGSIES'. I turned to ChatGPT for assistance in crafting a backronym, and through an iterative process of requests and refinements, we arrived at "Metric for Understanding Game, Given Sporting Individual's Effectiveness & Size." This outcome exceeded my expectations, offering a creative and fitting acronym that I might not have developed independently. The detailed conversation for this can be viewed at: https://chat.openai.com/share/68c7f4e4-04c5-486f-855a-fe2dcfc703da

A similar iterative approach was necessary for the development of charts. When people have seen the charts in this book, they often inquire about the specific prompts I used. However, no chart was the product of a single prompt. Every chart began as a draft created by ChatGPT, which was then improved through a series of back-and-forth interactions. This process is a testament to the dynamic and collaborative nature of working with ChatGPT, where the initial output is just the starting point for further refinement and improvement. To see what the process looks like, you can see one of my convos with ChatGPT here: https://chat.openai.com/share/2b09f9e1-9118-4445-80d5-681f0eaace7a.

Appendix 2: Math in Book

MUGGSIES formula

This is a 3-step process.

1) Assume that basketball ability can be broken down into a weighted average of two components: height and everything else. (This turns out to fit the data quite well.)

Normalized Basketball Ability = HeightContribution * Normalized Height + (1-HeightContribution)*Normalized Non-Height Basketball Ability

For every position on the court, find weights that would lead to height distributions as we see in the NBA. (These weights vary from height contributing 15 % towards overall ability for point guards to 64 % for centers.)

2) Simulate overall Normalized Basketball Ability. Assume only those with overall ability above 4 make the NBA and that those with higher overall ability have higher WS/48. Find the function to translate overall basketball ability (standard deviations above the mean) to WS/48. The best fit is:

Normalized Basketball Ability = 4.0542+1.2566*(Win Shares/48)+20.6482*(Win Shares/48)^2

3) Back out, from a player's WS/48, Height, and Position, his Normalized Non-Height Basketball Ability.

The total formula is:

MUGGSIES=$(4.0542+1.2566\times(WS/48)+20.6482\times(WS/48)^2-h$
$\times(Ht.$ in Inches$-70)/3)/$sqrt$(1-h^2)$
Where h = 0.8 for a C; 0.69 for a PF; 0.61 for a SF; 0.54 for a SG; and 0.39 for a PG

NATURE, NURTURE, & OTHER CONTRIBUTIONS TO SUCCESS.

1) Model athletic ability as a weighted average of nature, nurture, & other contributors.
2) Assume that those who reach the top of the field have the highest of that athletic ability. Calculate those above the cutoff in line with what percent of people in the population reach a certain pursuit – e.g., reaching the NBA.
3) Calculate the probability of a sibling or identical twin of someone who reaches the top also reaching the top based on cutoffs in step 2.
4) Simulate different weights of nature, nurture & others that match the family probabilities in that field.

The code to do this in R is as follows:

```
# Assume that ability is distributed normally; there are 3
components:
# - Genetic edge
# - Environmental edge
# - Random edge
# Define rareness as what percent of people have a skill
necessary to reach extreme performance.
# For example, the odds of someone being a professional
baseball player are about 1/11000, basketball is about 1/33000

rareness <- 1/11000
```

This is a simulation for how frequently we would expect identical twin siblings and other siblings to reach extreme performance.
You can pick different genetic and environmental weights that lead to identical twin sibling and other sibling odds that we see in reality.
For basketball, genetic weight around 0.8 and environmental weight around 0.15 worked well. For baseball, genetic weight around 0.3 and environmental weight around 0.45 were suitable.

```
genetic.weight <- 0.3
environmental.weight <- 0.45

draws <- 60000000

genetic.draw <- rnorm(draws, 0, 1)
environmental.draw <- rnorm(draws, 0, 1)
random.draw <- rnorm(draws, 0, 1)
brother.genetic.draw <- rnorm(draws, 0, 1)
brother.random.draw <- rnorm(draws, 0, 1)

brother <- 0.5
brother.next.cont <- sqrt(1 - 0.5^2)

zrequirement <- qnorm(1 - rareness, 0, 1)

random.weight <- 1 - genetic.weight - environmental.weight

dat <- as.data.frame(cbind(genetic.draw, environmental.draw, random.draw, brother.genetic.draw, brother.random.draw))

dat$total <- sqrt(genetic.weight) * dat$genetic.draw + sqrt(environmental.weight) * dat$environmental.draw + sqrt(random.weight) * dat$random.draw
```

```
dat <- dat[order(dat$total),]

dat$brothercontribution <- brother * sqrt(genetic.weight) *
dat$genetic.draw + sqrt(environmental.weight) *
dat$environmental.draw
dat$itcontribution <- sqrt(genetic.weight) * dat$genetic.draw +
sqrt(environmental.weight) * dat$environmental.draw

dat$brotherscore <- dat$brothercontribution +
brother.next.cont * sqrt(genetic.weight) *
dat$brother.genetic.draw + sqrt(random.weight) *
dat$brother.random.draw
dat$itscore <- dat$itcontribution + sqrt(random.weight) *
dat$brother.random.draw

dat$brotherneed <- (zrequirement - dat$brothercontribution)
dat$itneed <- (zrequirement - dat$itcontribution)

dat$prob.brother <- 1 - pnorm(dat$brotherneed, 0, sqrt(0.75 *
genetic.weight + random.weight))
dat$prob.it <- 1 - pnorm(dat$itneed, 0, sqrt(random.weight))

dat.lim <- dat[(dat$total >= zrequirement),]
dat.lim$it.yes <- 0
dat.lim$it.yes[(dat.lim$itscore >= zrequirement)] <- 1
dat.lim$brother.yes <- 0
dat.lim$brother.yes[(dat.lim$brotherscore >= zrequirement)] <-
1
it.odds <- mean(dat.lim$prob.it)
it.ratio <- it.odds / rareness
brother.odds <- mean(dat.lim$prob.brother)
brother.ratio <- brother.odds / rareness
```

The output is the odds of a same-sex sibling and identical twin of someone who achieved the accomplishment also achieving the accomplishment.

Notes for Charts & Images

Charts

Likelihood of American Males of Every Height Reaching the NBA:

- For NBA Players born between 1970 and 1999.
- Height data from Basketball Reference.
- Men born in the United States during that period from Our World in Data
- Men of every height estimated using a simulation, with height distributed normally with mean 5'10" and standard deviation of 3 inches.

Relationship Between Height and Vertical Leap of NBA Players:

- Data from the NBA Combine, years 2000-2022.
- Download link: https://www.kaggle.com/datasets/marcusfern/nba-draft-combine

Relationship Between Height and Slowness of NBA Players:

- Data from the NBA Combine, years 2000-2022.
- Download link: https://www.kaggle.com/datasets/marcusfern/nba-draft-combine

Relationship Between Height and FT % of NBA Players:

- Includes all NBA players who have at least 100 free throw attempts.
- Data from Basketball Reference.

Top 10 Height-Adjusted Players in History:

- Data on WS/48 and Height from Basketball Reference.

Where NBA Legends Rank in Basketball Ability, Taking Out Height:

- Data on WS/48 and Height from Basketball Reference.
- Athletic ranking of basketball ability: https://theathletic.com/3137873/2022/02/23/the-nba-75-the-top-75-nba-players-of-all-time-from-mj-and-lebron-to-lenny-wilkens/

Where NBA Players Have Come From:

- Place of birth data from Basketball Reference.

NBA Players per Million Births:

- Among NBA players born between 1970 and 1999.
- Place of birth data from Basketball Reference.
- Births data from Our World of Data.

Average Male Height:

- Data from Wikipedia.

NBA Players per Million Births, by Average Male Height of Country:

- Among NBA players born in the 1970s or 1980s.
- Place of birth data from Basketball Reference.
- Births data from Our World of Data.
- Average male height data from Wikipedia.

Foreign-Born Percent of NBA Players, by Height Bucket:

- For players who started their NBA career from 2000 onwards.
- Data from Basketball Reference.

"Short" NBA Players per Million Male Births, by Basketball Interest:

- Basketball Interest measured by Google Trends using the topic search "Basketball."

The Twins of the NBA:

- All data comes from news stories.
- The fact that Carl and Charles Thomas are identical twins was found via a LinkedIn conversation with Charles Thomas.

Percentage of Same-Sex Siblings Who Are Identical Twins:

- All Olympic data was provided by Bill Mallon.
- NBA, NFL, and MLB data from publicly available sources.

Increased Odds of Achieving This, if you have a father who achieved it:

- Calculations are from my article here: https://www.nytimes.com/2015/03/22/opinion/sunday/seth-stephens-davidowitz-just-how-nepotistic-are-we.html.
- Calculations for professor, elementary school teacher, and janitor are from here: https://www.nytimes.com/interactive/2017/11/22/upshot/the-jobs-youre-most-likely-to-inherit-from-your-mother-and-father.html

Likelihood of Reaching the NBA by Socio-Economics of County of Birth:

- Data source:
  https://www.nytimes.com/2013/11/03/opinion/sunday/in-the-nba-zip-code-matters.html

Black NBA Players vs. Black Population:

- Data source:
  https://www.nytimes.com/2013/11/03/opinion/sunday/in-the-nba-zip-code-matters.html

Probability of Being Incarcerated by Parental Income:

- Data source: Opportunity Insights.

The Moment Proves Too Big:

- Clutch shooting and non-clutch shooting data from NBA.com.

Ice in their Veins:

- Clutch shooting and non-clutch shooting data from NBA.com.

Where NBA Players Went to College:

- Data from Basketball Reference.

Probability of Being Drafted, by High School Recruit Rank & College Attended:

- Among top 100 high school players, 1998-2013.
- Data source: https://data.world/the-pudding/hype

NBA Legends with Legendarily Big Hands:

- NBA player data from here:
  https://howtheyplay.com/team-sports/14-NBA-Players-With-the-Most-Impressive-Hand-Sizes
- Average adult male hand size data from here:
  https://censusatschool.ca/data-results/2004-05/average-hand-span-age/

Performance Above or Below Expected Draft Size, by Hand Width:

- Hand size data for 2000-2022 from here:
  https://www.kaggle.com/datasets/marcusfern/nba-draft-combine
- Draft and WS/48 data from Basketball Reference.
- Performance above or below expected is based on a regression model predicting WS/48 based on a 5th-degree polynomial of draft pick.

Performance of Draft Picks Who Attended College & Didn't:

- Among draft picks between 1990 and 2015 (Result is robust to using different periods.)
- All data from Basketball Reference.

Effects of Physical Attributes on Blocks Per Minute in the NBA:

- All physical attributes data from 2000-2022 from here:
  https://www.kaggle.com/datasets/marcusfern/nba-draft-combin.
- Blocks per minute data from Basketball Reference.

Vertical Leap vs. Standing Leap:

- Data from 2000-2022 from here: https://www.kaggle.com/datasets/marcusfern/nba-draft-combine

Average WS/48 by Pick Group & Recruit Rank:

- Data for 1998-2013.
- Recruit data from here: https://data.world/the-pudding/hype
- WS/48 and draft pick data from Basketball Reference.

How a Player's Stats Contribute to His Wins:

- Multivariate regression predicting WS/48 on points per minute, rebounds per minute, assists per minute, blocks per minute, steals per minute, field goal percentage, free throw percentage, and three point percentage. All variables scaled.
- Data from Basketball Reference.

How a Player's Stats Contribute to His Salary:

- Multivariate regression predicting log salary.
- NBA Salary data from HoopsHype.
- NBA Statistics data from Basketball Reference.

How a Player's Stats Contribute to his Social Media Fans:

- Multivariate regression predicting log Facebook fans.
- Data collected from Facebook's advertising platform in 2017.
- NBA statistics data from Basketball Reference.

Best Coaches of the Modern Era:

- Data from Basketball Reference.

How much coaches influence outcomes:

- Research Study here:
  https://www.science.org/doi/10.1126/sciadv.abe3404

Change in Percent of Time the Same Player Will Pass:

- Regress percent of time passing ball on drive on coach fixed effects and player fixed effects.
- Data for percent of time passing ball on drive from NBA.com.
- Data for which coaches players played for in given year from Basketball Reference.

Images

Cover
- Created by Fiverr user

No Court for Short Men
- Created on MidJourney with the prompt: "An extremely tall NBA player holding a ball away from a short guy"

Missing LeBrons
- Created on MidJourney with the prompt: "Weak LeBron James with no tattoos working as a rice farmer in India" – Note: MidJourney didn't succeed in making him weak or removing tattoos.

The Basketball Genes
- Created with Dalle

Like Father, Like Son
- Created on MidJourney with the prompt: "A black son stands on his dad's shoulders and dunks a

ball." – Note: MidJourney didn't exactly create this but produced a related result.

Who is a Choker
- Created by Fiverr user

Can You Beat the Draft
- Created with Dalle

On Coaches

- Created by Fiverr user

Sources

"Top 10 Basketball Players of All Time": "NBA 75: Top 75 NBA Players of All Time, from MJ and LeBron to Lenny Wilkens." *The Athletic*. February 23, 2022.

"Thabeet Was Born to an Oxford-Educated Architect": Winn, Luke. "Hasheem the Dream." *Sports Illustrated Vault*. November 17, 2008.

"Why Basketball Is So Popular in the Baltic States": "The Godfathers of Lithuanian Basketball." *FIBA basketball*.

"Why Basketball Is So Popular in the Former Yugoslavia": "The Balkans Basketball Boom." *The Ringer*, February 21, 2023.

"When Kobe Bryant Was a Kid": Newsham, Gavin. "How Growing Up in Italy for 7 Years Turned Kobe Bryant into a Star." *New York Post*, January 8, 2022.

"When Steph Curry Was a Kid": "Stephen Curry's Childhood and How He Started His NBA Career." *Sportsmanor*.

"When Jalen Brunson Was a Toddler": "Jalen Brunson's Childhood Memories Reveal His Unflappable Spirit." *Dallas News*, April 19, 2022.

"When Klay Thompson Was a Kid": Gartland, Dan. "Klay Thompson and Kevin Love Were Little League Teammates." *Sports Illustrated*, October 27, 2021.

"Nikola Jokic Plays Basketball as if It's Water Polo": Cacciola, Scott. "Nikola Jokic: The Water Polo World's Favorite N.B.A. Player." *The New York Times*, September 22, 2020.

"A 'Kind' Environment": "David Epstein on Kind and Wicked Learning Environments." *Driverless Crocodile*.

"Stuntin' Like His Daddy": Spears, Marc J. "Stuntin' Like His Daddy: How Devin Booker's Father Paved His Path to the NBA." *Andscape*.

"Joshua Kjerulf Dubrow and Jimi Adams": "Hoop Inequalities: Race, Class and Family Structure Background and the Odds of Playing in the National Basketball Association." *International Review for the Sociology of Sport* 47, no. 1 (2010).

"Wrenn": Stephens-Davidowitz, Seth. *Everybody Lies: Big Data, New Data, and What the Internet Can Tell Us About Who We Really Are*. Dey Street Books, 2017.

"Most Players Don't Really Love Basketball": "Rockets' James Harden: 'Most Players Don't Really Love Basketball'." Rockets Wire, *USA Today*, February 9, 2019.

"Something That I'm Good At": Chaudhary, Aikansh. "Nikola Jokic: Basketball Is Not The Main Thing In My Life, It's Something That I'm Good At." *Fadeaway World*.

"O'Neal Admitted There Was Some Truth to This and That He Never Worked Hard in Practice": "Shaq Interview: I Never Worked Hard in Practice." YouTube, uploaded by Graham Bensinger.

"Warren Buffett": Stephens-Davidowitz, Seth. *Everybody Lies: Big Data, New Data, and What the Internet Can Tell Us About Who We Really Are*. Dey Street Books, 2017.

"The Average Harvard Grad Makes $123,000": Stephens-Davidowitz, Seth. *Everybody Lies: Big Data, New Data, and What the Internet Can Tell Us About Who We Really Are*. Dey Street Books, 2017.

"Alan Krueger and Stacy Dale": Dale, Stacy B., and Alan B. Krueger. "Estimating the Effects of College Characteristics over the Career Using Administrative Earnings Data." *The Journal of Human Resources* 49, no. 2 (Spring 2014): 323-358.

"Raj Chetty Used Even Better Data": Chetty, Raj, David J. Deming, and John N. Friedman. "Diversifying Society's Leaders? The Determinants and Causal Effects of Admission to Highly Selective Private Colleges." Working Paper 31492. National Bureau of Economic Research, July 2023.

"Consider Paul Millsap": Boatright, T. Scott. "LA Tech Hall of Famer - Paul Millsap." LA Tech Athletics. Louisiana Tech University.

"He Went with Michael": Martinez, Jose. "Kobe Bryant Lakers SG Wishes He Had Michael Jordan Hands." *Complex*. Complex Media, Inc.

"The Secret of Basketball": Simmons, Bill. *The Book of Basketball: The NBA According to The Sports Guy*. Ballantine Books, 2009.

"Ramzy Al-Amine": Al-Amine, Ramzy. "Quantifying the Contribution of NBA Coaches Using Fixed Effects." Towards Data Science. Medium.

"Found That NBA Coaches Have More Influence on the Outcome of Games Than Coaches in Any Other Sport": Berry, Christopher, and Anthony Fowler. "How Much Do Coaches Matter." Sloan Sports Conference.

"Gregg Popovich": Coyle, Daniel. *The Culture Code: The Secrets of Highly Successful Groups*. Kindle Edition. Bantam, 2018.

"Shawn Bradley": Ebbert, Mark T. W., Ryan H. Miller, Meganne Ferrel, et al. "Common DNA Variants Accurately Rank an Individual of Extreme Height." *International Journal of Genomics*, vol. 2018, September 4, 2018.

Praise for *Who Makes the NBA*

"I love reading Seth Stephens-Davidowitz modern take on what it takes to make it in the NBA. Having lived it, it's a fun way to look at beating the odds. I certainly feel lucky to have played 13 years in the NBA after reading about the seemingly rare chances that I would rise above the odds. I think you will enjoy learning about the unique statistical profile of what it takes to make it to the NBA."
-- Shane Battier, two-time NBA champion basketball player for the Miami Heat

"A fascinating analysis of what it takes to reach and excel in the NBA – and a clever use of artificial intelligence."
-- Larry Fitzgerald, 11x Pro Bowler for Arizona Cardinals; minority owner of Phoenix Suns.

"Couldn't put this book down....a truly fascinating and data-driven guide to the world of NBA basketball, filled with unexpected insights. Think Malcolm Gladwell goes one-on-one with LeBron James, and you've got Seth Stephens-Davidowitz!"
-- Oz "the Mentalist" Pearlman

"trailblazing ... ground-breaking"
-- James Altucher, best-selling author of *Choose Yourself*

"I really liked this book."
-- Tyler Cowen, Marginal Revolution

About the Author

Seth Stephens-Davidowitz is a data scientist, economist, and author. His 2017 book *Everybody Lies* was a *New York Times* bestseller and an *Economist* Book of the Year. His 2022 book *Don't Trust Your Gut* was excerpted in the *Atlantic*, *Wired*, and the *New York Times*. He has worked as a Google data scientist, a contributing op-ed writer for the *New York Times*, and a visiting lecturer at the Wharton School. He has a BA in philosophy from Stanford and a PhD in economics from Harvard. He lives in Brooklyn and is a passionate fan of the Knicks, Mets, Jets, and Leonard Cohen.

18855038R00069